ABSOLUTE JUSTICE

The History and Legacy of Agatha Christie's And Then There Were None

CHRIS CHAN

As always, to my parents, Drs. Carlyle and Patricia Chan
And to my Aunt Cheryl and Uncle Raynold

Contents

Introduction

"I read a story once—about two judges that came to a small American town—from the Supreme Court. They administered justice—Absolute Justice. Because—they didn't come from this world at all..."

   —Vera Claythorne, And Then There Were None[1]

And Then There Were None is the world's bestselling mystery novel, written by the world's bestselling novelist. Agatha Christie (1890–1976) produced scores of books, short stories, and plays over more than fifty-five years as a professional writer, shattering publishing and box-office records along the way. Few authors have achieved this much success, let alone maintained it for so long. While other prolific crime writers have gone out of print and faded into obscurity, Christie remains a cultural force to be reckoned with nearly half a century after she passed away. Her books have been translated into over a hundred languages, and all of her novels are still in print in English-speaking countries. The twenty-first century has seen an explosion in adaptations of her work for film, television, stage, and radio, some of which have won or been nominated for major awards.

A commonly-cited estimate from the *Guinness Book of World Records* claims that Christie has sold over two billion books, half in English, half in other languages combined, and approximately one hundred million copies of *And Then There Were None* alone have been purchased since its publication in 1939. With over ninety books to her credit, it's surprising that just one novel makes up a disproportionate five percent of her total sales.[2]

As a global bestseller with widespread recognition, *And Then There Were None* is a cultural phenomenon. Few other novels have had such a widespread readership, and for so long. Like many influential creative works,

And Then There Were None has developed a story of its own, reaching far beyond the confines of a book's binding. It has been adapted and parodied, and it has shaped literary boundaries from the crime genre and beyond.

In his critical overview of Christie, *A Talent to Deceive*, Robert Barnard called *And Then There Were None* "Probably the best-known Christie, and justifiably among the most popular."[3] Author Gillian Flynn called *And Then There Were None* "the book that changed my life," saying that, "[Christie] was the first author that I read from the grown-up section in the library. The realization that every character in that book was evil slowly dawned on my 12-year-old brain. I realized there were different gradations of evil and it blew my mind. I gobbled her up. It made me want to be a mystery writer, the idea that you can be entranced by bad characters."[4] *And Then There Were None* is often the first—or one of the first—Christie novels people read, and even if they haven't actually read it, they've probably read or seen something influenced by it.

And Then There Were None has been published under multiple titles over the decades. For the purposes of this study, the book will always be referred to as *And Then There Were None*, save for references to an adaptation using a different title.

Despite its massive fame, the details of *And Then There Were None's* broader cultural impact are rarely discussed. Though many books have been written on Christie's life and works, until now there has never been a full-length study focusing on just one of her novels. This monograph explores not only the novel *And Then There Were None*, but its adaptations, impact on the genre, and historical impact. *And Then There Were None* is one of the very few books that has taken on a life of its own, and the story of its mark on the world is as interesting as Christie's original tale.

A Note on Spoilers

Though spoilers on the content of *And Then There Were None* and its adaptations are unavoidable in an in-depth study, there will also be some spoilers for other works as well, though they have been crafted to be as oblique as possible, except in cases of direct comparison. Please read with caution.

[1] Agatha Christie, *And Then There Were None*. HarperCollins, 1939, 2009 ed. Kindle.

[2] Christie, *And Then There Were None*. Due to inadequate sales tracking, no standard global means of collecting worldwide sales statistics, bootleg copies of Christie's work for which she received no royalties, and the chaos resulting from WWII, it is impossible to produce an exact number of sales, so this number ought to be viewed as an educated estimate. For much of her life, *The Murder of Roger Ackroyd* was Christie's bestselling novel, but *And Then There Were None* has since overtaken it.

[3] Robert Barnard, *A Talent to Deceive: An Appreciation of Agatha Christie*, Revised and Updated Edition (Mysterious Press, 1987), 203.

[4] Gillian Flynn, "Gillian Flynn: 'Agatha Christie blew my mind. Every character was evil," *The Guardian*, July 6, 2018, https://www.theguardian.co m/books/2018/jul/06/books-that-made-me-gillian-flynn.

I

PART ONE: The Book

Chapter One

The Plot

While it is normally verboten to reveal critical plot points and the solution to mystery stories, as this is a critical study of a famous crime novel, a full discussion of the narrative is necessary for a thorough analysis of *And Then There Were None*. In any event, as this book is directed towards fans of Christie's legendary work, most readers ought to have read the book, or at least have seen an adaptation of it, but this summary ought to refresh the memories of anybody who might need it. This is, at least, a more justified venue for spoilers than the original promotional material provided by the publisher Collins during the initial printing, which went so far as to spoil the entire plot of the novel, much to Christie's outrage!

As *And Then There Were None* opens, eight people are on their way to Soldier Island for a brief getaway. They are largely strangers to each other, and while some of them believe that they have been invited by old friends, the others are under the impression that they have been hired for a job. The guests are retired judge Justice Wargrave, the governess turned teacher Vera Claythorne, down-on-his-luck adventurer Philip Lombard, the deeply religious and judgmental Emily Brent, lonely military man General Macarthur, successful physician Doctor Armstrong, amoral and hedonistic Tony Marston, and private detective William Henry Blore, who is adopting the alias of a South African named Davis.

Soldier Island, located off the coast of Devon, has a reputation for being bought and sold repeatedly, but its current owner is supposed to be a Mr. Ulick Norman Owen, though there are rumors that this is just a cover for the true owner, which gossip states might be a film star or even a member of the Royal Family. Seven of the invitees (the latecomer, Dr. Armstrong, is ferried over separately after the others) are taken to Soldier Island by the boatman Fred Narracott. The boat ride to the island is fairly quick, though without a reliable vessel, it is impossible to travel back to the mainland.

The island is staffed by the married couple, Mr. and Mrs. Rogers, and the guests are informed that their hosts will arrive soon. The house is large, modern, and comfortable, and though the guests feel a bit awkward around people they do not know, it seems like it might be a pleasant stay.

As the guests settle into the island, the reader is provided with some brief glimpses into the minds of each character and learns that most of them have secrets and troubled pasts. A set of ten china soldiers sits upon the dining room table, and the nursery rhyme "Ten Little Soldiers" is framed in every bedroom. The rhyme is as follows:

TEN LITTLE SOLDIERS

Ten Little Soldier Boys went out to dine;
One choked his little self and then there were nine.
Nine Little Soldier Boys stayed up very late;
One overslept himself and then there were eight.
Eight Little Soldier Boys travelling in Devon;
One said he'd stay there and then there were seven.
Seven Little Soldier Boys chopping up sticks;
One chopped himself in halves and then there were six.
Six Little Soldier Boys playing with a hive;
A bumblebee stung one and then there were five.
Five Little Soldier Boys going in for law;
One got in Chancery and then there were four.
Four Little Soldier Boys going out to sea;
A red herring swallowed one and then there were three.
Three Little Soldier Boys walking in the Zoo;

A big bear hugged one and then there were two.
Two Little Soldier Boys sitting in the sun;
One got frizzled up and then there was one.
One Little Soldier Boy left all alone;
He went and hanged himself and then there were none.

Dinner passes amicably, but the tone of the evening changes dramatically when a condemnatory voice, previously recorded and played on a phonograph, accuses each of the ten people in the house of murder.

The characters are affected in various ways by the accusations. Most angrily, tearfully, sternly, or indignantly deny any wrongdoing. One refuses to respond, and two confess without showing any remorse. Indeed, none of them outwardly display any contrition or take responsibility for their actions, though brief glimpses into a couple of the characters' private thoughts reveal some guilt.

Judge Wargrave leads an inquiry, and after Mrs. Rogers is given a fortifying drink and sent to bed, the other nine characters compare notes and quickly realize that they were all brought to the island under false pretenses of either being invited by friends or by being offered jobs. Most of the official invitations to the island mentioned either a Ulick Norman Owen or an Una Nancy Owen, though Marston's was ostensibly from his pal Badger Berkeley, Wargrave claimed his was from his friend Lady Constance Culmington, the messy signature on Miss Brent's note was interpreted as that of a woman named "Oliver," and Lombard was hired verbally by the agent Isaac Morris without an employer's name being mentioned. Blore's deception is unmasked, and henceforth he is referred to by his real name. Wargrave realizes that the missing host and hostess are both named U.N. Owen, a play on the word "Unknown." Thoroughly unsettled, the guests all wish to leave immediately, but Rogers informs them that there is no boat on the island, and they have no choice but to wait for Fred Narracott to return in the morning.

Only Tony Marston wishes to stay and investigate. When chastised, he laughingly sips his whiskey and soda, and immediately starts choking. Dr. Armstrong pronounces him dead and detects cyanide in his drink. The stunned guests agree that it must have been a suicide, all too shaken up to suggest a more sinister explanation. Everybody retires for the night, though most of the characters wrestle with their memories and unsettled consciences.

The next morning, Armstrong is awakened by a distraught Rogers. Mrs. Rogers has died in her sleep. There are no signs of violence on the body, and though the exact cause of death cannot be determined without an autopsy, Mrs. Rogers' death is theorized to have been caused by either heart failure or by ingesting poison, perhaps an overdose of sleeping medication.

Fred Narracott has not arrived on schedule, and of the remaining guests, only General Macarthur seems at peace. Armstrong and Lombard start discussing the situation and realize that the two deaths on the island match the nursery rhyme hanging in all of their rooms. Additionally, the set of ten china figurines is reduced by one every time a guest dies, as two soldiers are now missing. Deducing that the killer is hiding on the island, the pair, along with Blore, begin a thorough search, though they find no evidence of an eleventh person anywhere, and start to wonder if the two deceased individuals were not actually murdered, but instead died of suicide or natural causes. These doubts are permanently silenced when the General is found bludgeoned to death.

After a quick discussion, Wargrave concludes that they are being hunted by U.N. Owen as punishment for the murders they were accused of committing. Wargrave agrees with Armstrong, Lombard, and Blore that the killer is on the island, but is not an eleventh person. U.N. Owen is one of the seven surviving individuals. Further questioning proves that none of the guests can be cleared of culpability for any of the three murders, and in a new atmosphere of tense suspicion, all of the characters have an uneasy evening, as they each confide in the individuals they think least likely to be U.N. Owen, and start to wrestle with their own long-suppressed guilt.

When the guests' second full day on the island dawns, they are suddenly without a servant when Rogers is found dead from an axe wound to the head. More suspicions and accusations follow, and most of the guests start to crack in various ways from the strain. The tension rises even higher after lunch, when Emily Brent is slain by a hypodermic injection of poison. The deaths continue to match the nursery rhyme, and another china figurine vanishes with each killing.

Earlier, Blore noticed that Lombard possessed a revolver, but when the surviving guests attempt to retrieve his weapon from his room, it is missing. This leads to an unsuccessful search of the house for the gun, though the guests gather up the remaining medicines and poisons that might be used against them and lock them away. By this point, emotions are frayed, and the characters are mentally exhausted, both from the guilt they feel over the crimes they thought they had gotten away with and by the looming threat of death. The power has gone out due to the electric generator being neglected after the death of Rogers, so their third night on the island is illuminated by candlelight.

The five remaining guests spend most of the evening sitting around and staring at each other suspiciously, until Vera retreats to her bedroom. Once there, she feels a cold sensation smelling of the sea against her face, and screams. Lombard, Blore, and Armstrong rush to her aid and discover that someone has hung a large clump of seaweed from a hook on her ceiling. Once everybody settles down, they realize that Wargrave is missing. They find him in the living room, shot in the head.

After everybody goes to bed, Blore hears a figure walking through the corridor in the middle of the night. A quick search leads him to realize that Armstrong is the only one not in his room. Lombard, who has found his revolver returned to his room, joins Blore in the hunt for the doctor, while Vera shelters in her locked bedroom. Blore and Lombard are unable to find Armstrong, though they observe that only three china figures remain on the table.

The next morning, Lombard and Blore are very suspicious of each other, though Vera is convinced that Armstrong is the killer and is still alive. As the weather has cleared, the trio decides to try using a mirror and the sun to signal to the mainland for help. After a while, Blore returns to the house for a meal, and Vera and Lombard rush back when they hear a gigantic thud. Once they reach the mansion, they find Blore dead, his head crushed by a large marble clock shaped like a bear.

Convinced that Armstrong is alive and out to murder them, Vera and Lombard continue their search for the doctor. To their horror, they find his drowned body washed up on the beach, and they both conclude that the other is U.N. Owen.

Under the pretext of dragging Armstrong's body above the high-water mark, Vera snatches Lombard's revolver away from him. When Lombard attempts to wrest back his gun, she fatally shoots him.

Dazed and relieved, Vera wanders back to the house, only to discover a noose hanging from the hook in her room with a chair underneath it. Suddenly wracked by guilt, Vera's will to survive breaks down, and feeling the sudden compulsion to atone for her crime, hangs herself.

The narrative jumps forward a bit as two detectives, Sir Thomas Legge and Inspector Maine, discuss the case. Ten bodies have been found on the island, and Isaac Morris, the man who managed the financial arrangements to set up the island for the guests, has fatally overdosed from sleeping drugs. Legge and Maine observe that some of the guests left notes and diary entries regarding the events, allowing them to figure out the order of the first six deaths. (Notably, neither detective makes the connection to the rhyme.) The forensic evidence proves that none of the remaining four could have been the last one alive on the island—Armstrong's body was dragged beyond the water line, Blore was physically and psychologically incapable of crushing his head with the marble clock, the revolver was found in the house far from Lombard, and the chair Vera stood on to hang herself was replaced against the wall.

The police are utterly baffled as to how the crimes could have been committed, and the case is only solved by the lucky chance of a fishing trawler discovering the murderer's confession, rolled up in a sealed bottle and tossed into the sea. In this manuscript, Wargrave describes his own homicidal tendencies that have been tempered by his innate sense of justice. While his lifelong fantasy was to commit a perfect, elaborate murder, he recoiled at the thought of taking an innocent life. Upon hatching the idea of only killing murderers who got away with it, he launched an investigation to find ten people who were responsible for other individuals' deaths, yet who escaped punishment (Morris is Wargrave's tenth victim, having caused the death of a young woman by getting her addicted to drugs). Having done so, Wargrave bought and set up Soldier Island through Morris, invited all of his victims-to-be, and gave Morris poisoned medication before leaving for the island.

Wargrave then killed the others one by one, having planned out his crimes well ahead of time. After stealing Lombard's revolver, he hid it in a food tin, which went unsearched as the others assumed it was sealed. Armstrong trusted Wargrave and accepted the judge's plan to fake his own death in order to draw out the killer. The others accepted the doctor's pronouncement that Wargrave was deceased, and the last four deaths went exactly as Wargrave had hoped. Interested in psychological manipulation, he wanted to make one of his last two victims kill the other (he correctly figured that Vera could outwit Lombard) and then be sufficiently traumatized to commit suicide given subtle provocation.

After cleaning up the crime scenes to make sure that the guilt could not be pinned on any of the others, Wargrave returned to his room and shot himself, using a handkerchief to prevent leaving fingerprints, and his elastic eyeglass cord was attached to the gun to propel it far away from him after his suicide. It worked, and the police failed to suspect that he had taken his own life. Had Wargrave not written a confession, and the fishing ship had not retrieved the message in a bottle, the case would likely have gone unsolved forever.[1]

[1] Christie, *And Then There Were None.*

Chapter Two

The Victims

"Ladies and gentlemen! Silence, please!...

You are charged with the following indictments:

Edward George Armstrong, that you did upon the 14th day of March, 1925, cause the death of Louisa Mary Clees.

Emily Caroline Brent, that upon the 5th November, 1931, you were responsible for the death of Beatrice Taylor.

William Henry Blore, that you brought about the death of James Stephen Landor on October 10th, 1928.

Vera Elizabeth Claythorne, that on the 11th day of August, 1935, you killed Cyril Ogilvie Hamilton.

Philip Lombard, that upon a date in February, 1932, you were guilty of the death of twenty-one men, members of an East African tribe.

John Gordon Macarthur, that on the 4th of January, 1917, you deliberately sent your wife's lover, Arthur Richmond, to his death.

Anthony James Marston, that upon the 14th day of November last, you were guilty of the murder of John and Lucy Combes.

Thomas Rogers and Ethel Rogers, that on the 6th of May, 1929, you brought about the death of Jennifer Brady.

Lawrence John Wargrave, that upon the 10th day of June, 1930, you were guilty of the murder of Edward Seton.

Prisoners at the bar, have you anything to say in your defence?"[1]

In Christie novels, some victims loom larger than others. The titular Roger Ackroyd is said to be crime fiction's most famous homicide victim. Some of her most prominent murdered characters, such as those killed off in *Murder on the Orient Express*, *Hercule Poirot's Christmas*, and *Appointment with Death*, are malignant and destructive embodiments of evil. Others are extremely likable and sympathetic, causing the reader to demand vengeance for their untimely demises. Some are deeply flawed and complex characters, and others have no personality at all, existing on the page solely for the purpose of being killed off early in the book.

Several of the characters murdered before the events of *And Then There Were None* are essentially nonentities. Readers are told nothing about John and Lucy Combes, two innocent children who were run over by Anthony Marston's reckless driving, though, as they were children, their deaths seem all the more tragic to many readers who see young lives cut short. The Rogers' employer, Jennifer Brady, is known only as a very ill woman of means, reliant on the servants who possibly resented her and definitely desired the money she promised them in her will. Doctor Armstrong's victim, Louisa Mary Clees, is a woman who needed a simple operation and just happened to come under the scalpel of the wrong doctor at the wrong time. The twenty-two members of an African tribe that Lombard abandoned? Nothing is known about these poor people, not even their names.

A few others are only slightly more fleshed out as individuals, though what is revealed about their lives is thought-provoking. Blore's victim, James Landor, was an innocent man who got framed for a serious crime because the real criminals paid off Blore and ordered him to use Landor as a patsy for the London and Commercial bank robbery. Wrongly accused of beating the night watchman unconscious, Landor, who was in fragile health, was sentenced to a lifetime of penal servitude and passed away after just a year of hard labor. It is not clear why the gang who worked with Blore chose to make Landor their fall guy. Perhaps he was just conveniently situated, and it was easy for Blore to place Landor in the frame through carefully crafted perjury. Landor had a wife and teenaged daughter, but nothing is known about what happened to them.

Comparably, readers know little about Edward Seton. It's clear that he is incredibly charming and personable, but he is also a cold-blooded killer. Not much more background is provided on Beatrice Taylor. We know she had a physical relationship with a man who wasn't prepared to marry or even assist her and her child (though we cannot know for sure if it was consensual), and her parents also rejected her after they learned of her condition. As for Arthur Richmond, he was a personable young man who was able to charm Leslie Macarthur, a woman who found most fellows dull. Though he was guilty of adultery, nothing is known about whether he wrestled with his conscience when he had an affair with the wife of his commanding officer.

The victim readers know the most about is Cyril Hamilton, the boy under Vera's care. He is the only one whom the reader actually sees in flashbacks, as opposed to brief descriptions in their killers' thoughts and dialogue, if anything at all. She sees him as whiny and spoiled, but this may be colored by her own desire for the inheritance his existence denies his uncle. After all, there must be plenty of good and charm in the lad if his uncle Hugo was so fond of him. Without Vera's commentary, all readers see is a boy who wants to swim and have an adventure by going farther than he is supposed to go. In short, he's a perfectly normal kid who had the bad luck to have a horrific governess.

With the exception of Seton, none of these characters committed any crimes or did anything to justify their fates. Two of them violated sexual mores, but their actions were not capital crimes. Seton's death sentence was legal and justifiable, but the others were not.

Cyril Hamilton and Jennifer Brady were deliberately killed for expected profit, and Landor and the East African tribesmen were both left to unpleasant fates for career advancement and an improved chance of survival, respectively. Louise Clees and the Combs kids were victims of criminal negligence. Richmond's adulterous affair may have been morally objectionable, but did he have to pay for his sins with his life? As for Beatrice Taylor, she was driven to suicide after being chewed out by a self-righteous woman who filled her with guilt and left her with few promising options for her future.

The general innocence of most of these victims makes the actions of their killers all the more despicable, but in order to understand the minds of these murderers, each must be analyzed one by one.[2]

[1] Christie, *And Then There Were None*.

[2] Christie, *And Then There Were None*.

Chapter Three

Anthony Marston

How does one judge the man who feels no remorse? Should he be considered an inherently bad person, or is he simply the victim of some defect in his mental make-up beyond his control? In a book where nearly all of the characters are wracked with guilt brought about by the condemnation of their own consciences, Anthony Marston has not a twinge of shame for his crime.

Modern psychology might use terms like "sociopath" or "antisocial" to describe people like Marston, but are those really accurate? Less clinical terms are used by the killer when he dubs Marston "amoral." As the first to die on the island, the reader is given precious little time to study his mind, but readers are provided with brief snippets into his psyche. The quick snapshots of his mind show him taking great pleasure in fast driving, judging the other guests as not quite his type, and feeling relief at seeing the well-stocked bar on the island.

The primary motivating factor in Marston's life appears to be the pursuit of pleasure and thrills. He does not appear to have a profession, and it can be assumed that he's inherited enough wealth to live as a playboy, though his untitled status indicates that he's not a member of the aristocracy, so it's unclear how his family obtained its wealth. He enjoys fast cars and chides others for championing speed limits. Drinking and driving pose no concern to him, as he consumes a gin and ginger beer on the road to Soldier Island.

His life seems to consist mainly of social engagements with his friends. Not all of his pals are wealthy. Badger, the chum who supposedly got Marston invited to the island, is personally broke and apparently has found ways to survive by sponging off the hospitality of others.

Additionally, right before his death, Marston is the only one of the ten people on the island who wishes to stay and investigate what brought them there, declaring, "Whole thing's like a detective story. Positively thrilling."[1] He does not appear to have any particular sleuthing skills of his own, but he does consider their situation to be an exciting adventure. The potential danger to himself or the others does not dampen his enthusiasm. If anything, his excitement is heightened.

Marston does not appear to have a functioning conscience, but in fairness, he also never expresses any malice. Whereas some of the other guests on the island bore rancor against the people whose deaths they caused, or sought personal gain by the deaths, Marston never intended to kill anybody, but he is responsible for causing death due to negligence.

As U.N. Owen notes in the epilogue, Marston was selected from a group of similar offenders. This makes Marston the only character to actually go through the justice system for his crime, though the punishment— the suspension of his driving license for a year—was pitifully small when compared to the lives of two children being cut brutally short. Deaths caused while driving are unfortunately not rare, but Marston's case stood out due to, in Wargrave's words,

"his complete callousness and his inability to feel any responsibility for the lives he had taken," which "made him...a type dangerous to the community and unfit to live."[2]

Hearing the names of his victims announced on the gramophone record has no effect on Marston. The words "John and Lucy Combes" spark no memory, at least not immediately. He even growls, "Don't know what the damned fool was getting at!"[3] This is a rather shocking declaration, as virtually any other person who was responsible for the deaths of two children—even if it was purely accidental—would immediately recall this tragic event. Apparently, running over the kids had so little impact on him that it took several minutes of thinking to recall the event that the record referenced. Even after taking their lives, Marston could not be bothered to learn their names.

When speaking to the others, Marston has no tears of remorse, nor does he show any compassion for the Combes' parents. After being questioned as to what he meant by calling the incident "beastly bad luck," Marston declares that he was thinking about the endorsement (suspension) of his driver's license for a year, and it is only when pressed that he concedes that it was bad luck for the Combes children also.[4] There are no tears, no self-recrimination, and there is certainly no guilt in Marston's words. He sees their deaths as nothing more than an accident, one that is unfortunate mainly because it inconvenienced him personally.

Internally, Marston worries only about his personal amusements and is not bothered by factors like shame or responsibility. Physically, he is young and striking. Right after his death, he is described as "That young Norse God in the prime of his health and strength."[5] In his first appearance, his personal characteristics are said to be "six feet of well-proportioned body, his crisp hair, tanned face, and intensely blue eyes."[6] He is attractive to women, judging by the gazes he receives from the opposite sex, and his automobile, a Super Sports Dalmain, is also eye-catching.

Marston is somewhat observant, as he is able to track down a tray of alcoholic beverages with little difficulty, and he is also the one who first makes a verbal note of Owen's unusual first and middle names, though he is not the one who identifies the significance of the initials. He may behave foolishly, but there's no reason to think he is stupid, just reckless and self-obsessed.

His selection as the first victim on the island was deliberate, as Wargrave's plan was to allow the worst offenders to suffer extended periods of guilt and fear, as their survival instinct clashed with their growing realizations that they deserved punishment. Marston's being the initial victim to die not only reflected Wargrave's realization that Marston's mental make-up would have shielded him from the psychological torture that the others endured, but also, the sudden extinguishing of one of the youngest and healthiest members of the group served to make the specter of death all the more impactful on the others.

The means of his death, cyanide in his drink, was a swift demise, though not quite as "instantaneous" as the killer suggests.[7] After consuming a large dose of cyanide, death occurred in just a few seconds, though the choking death may have meant a brief, intense period of agonizing pain. It is unlikely that he felt any guilt or thought of anything but himself in his final moments. Marston, as the killer notes, "was a type born without that feeling of moral responsibility which most of us have."[8] Had he never come to Soldier Island, he would very likely have spent the rest of his life in the pursuit of self-gratification, and it is possible that his reckless driving could have caused the deaths of even more innocent people.

[1] Christie, *And Then There Were None.*

[2] Christie, *And Then There Were None.*

[3] Christie, *And Then There Were None.*

[4] Christie, *And Then There Were None.*

[5] Christie, *And Then There Were None.*

[6] Christie, *And Then There Were None.*

[7] Christie, *And Then There Were None.*

[8] Christie, *And Then There Were None.*

Chapter Four

Ethel Rogers

Of all of the ten central characters of *And Then There Were None*, the reader is provided with the least information about Mrs. Rogers. In a Christie novel that spends more time exploring the mental turmoil and streams of consciousness of its characters than the vast majority of her works, Mrs. Rogers is the only one of the ten where no insight is provided into her private thoughts. The glimpses into Marston's mind is brief—his thoughts on the weekend party, his disappointment over the other guests, and his delight at seeing a well-stocked table are all the reader is allowed to see—but these short passages are far more than what is revealed into Mrs. Rogers' mind.

Mrs. Rogers only factors into two brief scenes. In the first, Mrs. Rogers is presented entirely through Vera's eyes.

"Mrs. Rogers had a flat monotonous voice. Vera looked at her curiously. What a white bloodless ghost of a woman! Very respectable looking, with her hair dragged back from her face and her black dress. Queer light eyes that shifted the whole time from place to place.

Vera thought: "She looks frightened of her own shadow."

Yes, that was it—frightened!

She looked like a woman who walked in mortal fear..."[1]

If Mrs. Rogers' predominant character trait is fear, what is it that fills her with such apprehension? Is it worrying about the prospect of punishment for her and her husband being responsible for the death of their employer? Is the punishment she fears temporal or eternal? Or is it fear *of* her husband? As readers are not given any glimpses into the states of her mind or her marriage, one can only speculate.

Without any insights into Mrs. Rogers' psyche and since she never says a word to defend or incriminate herself regarding the accusation of murder, the reader never gets any definite knowledge as to the extent of her guilt. In the epilogue, the killer is positive that Mrs. Rogers only acquiesced in allowing her employer to die because her husband pressured her to let it happen. If this is indeed the case, it allows the reader to wonder as to the true extent of Mrs. Rogers' involvement. If she only participated in denying Mrs. Brady her medicine due to threats and pressure from her husband, then, depending on the extent of her husband's influence, her guilt may be mitigated somewhat. Unless her husband physically restrained her from administering the life-saving medication, and then blackmailed or browbeat her into keeping quiet by threatening to implicate or physically harm her, then Mrs. Rogers is indeed guilty of being an accomplice to causing Mrs. Brady's death by deliberate negligence. Knowing that she has her employer's death on her conscience, and that the possibility that repercussions might occur at some point, has warped Mrs. Rogers' whole demeanor.

In her second and final scene, Mrs. Rogers faints after hearing the accusatory gramophone record. While the other guests are concerned over her well-being, her husband is less worried about his wife's health and more fretful over what she might say. It can be safely inferred that he fears that his wife will confess to the murder of their employer. This indicates guilt on Rogers' part, as well as an indication that he sees his wife as a threat to his safety. Given these hints, it can safely be inferred that this was not a case of a Lady Macbeth-like woman pushing her husband into murder, but rather the other way around.

In the epilogue, the killer states that in his opinion, Mrs. Rogers "had acted very largely under the influence of her husband."[2] As the killer is shown to be correct about all of his other allegations throughout the book, and given the obviousness of Mrs. Rogers' mental distress, the reader can therefore act under the assumption that he is correct again in this case, and that Mrs. Rogers would never have fatally withheld Mrs. Brady's medication when left to her own devices. Whether her husband cajoled her into following his plan, or whether she was bullied into acquiescence, is unknown. No matter how her husband pressured her, Mrs. Rogers made a conscious choice to deny Mrs. Brady her medicine, committing an act that she knew was terribly wrong.

Mrs. Rogers' crime seems to have done her far more harm than good. While she and her husband received a small legacy for their work, it clearly was not enough to get them to leave domestic service. Apparently, the legacy was enough to commit murder for, but the reader is not provided with any information on just how much money was inherited, nor is there any clue what happened to it. Perhaps Mr. and Mrs. Rogers funneled their bequeathal into a business venture or other investment and lost it. Maybe it was less than they expected. It probably was not enough to support them for the rest of their lives in any event, but after Mrs. Brady's death, they lost their steady employment, and they were compelled to use an employment agency to help them find work, and they never found a comparably steady position with an employer who liked and trusted them. It is possible that the doctor who suspected homicidal negligence warned away potential employers. It is also within the bounds of likelihood that Mrs. Rogers' frightened demeanor, coupled with her husband's constant oversight and discreet bullying, unsettled employers, who decided not to hire the pair for long-term work.

The reader is told nothing about the decade of Mr. and Mrs. Rogers' lives between the murder and their brief tenure at Soldier Island, but unless misguided money-making schemes depleted their funds, it is likely that most, if not all, of their legacy was used up in living expenses as they waited for regular work. The job at Soldier Island may have been ostensibly lucrative enough to attract them, but as Christie's stage adaptation of the novel points out, there are distinct downsides to working on an island. One cannot slip away to see a film or take a quick escape to have a drink at a sociable pub. Essentially, one is a prisoner at one's workplace. Given the fact that the

Rogers were looking for work, they may have felt they had no choice but to take the job.

In essence, Mrs. Rogers' life was one of fear and guilt after allowing her employer to die, and of all the people on the island, she may have been the most aware of how badly her crime had ruined her life. Perhaps when she met her fate, there was a certain element of relief...

[1] Christie, *And Then There Were None.*

[2] Christie, *And Then There Were None.*

Chapter Five

General John Macarthur

Of all the guests on Soldier Island, it is the retired soldier who is the most accepting of his guilt and his ultimate fate. Once the guests start dying, the General makes no attempt to make a last stand to save his own life. He surrenders himself to his execution, content in the knowledge that he deserves what is coming to him.

As the story opens, the General is a lonely man. A widower, he is aware of a certain level of distancing between himself and his fellow comrades in arms. He attributes this to a rumor about him that is causing others to become uncomfortable in his presence, and though this rumor is not identified in the General's introductory scene, it is soon clear that many of the General's colleagues believe that he deliberately sent one of his own men to die in battle. Given the speed with which rumors can circulate, this explains how the killer learned about the General's background.

Unlike any of the other guests, the accusing record provides a clear motive for the General's crime. While the others are only provided with the name or names of their victims, Arthur Richmond is expressly identified as "your wife's lover."[1] No other guest's accusation comes with any sort of explanation for the action. When the guests respond to the record, the General must make a double denial. Not only does he proclaim his innocence as to the death of Richmond, but he also attempts to protect his wife's name from the allegation of adultery.

The General's defensive pose does not last for very long. Shaken by the sudden death of Marston, Macarthur retires to his room, deeply upset, and he lies in bed, reflecting on how he had liked Richmond and introduced him to his wife, Leslie. A mix-up in the letters Leslie sent to her husband and her paramour alerted the General to the affair, and after attempting to hide his true emotions, he eventually took an opportunity to send Richmond on a mission from which he would never return. Something in his manner or actions, though, might have alerted Armitage, a soldier under his command, that something was not quite right.

Macarthur's crime, unlike some of the others, was deliberately calculated in order to cause death. The General did not profit much from it. He returned home to his wife, but she never recovered from the grief of her lover's demise and passed away herself a few years later. The General retired from the army and withdrew quietly to a cottage in Devon, living out his days in increasing solitude as he grew increasingly aware of rumors about him.

It is notable that the General is inconsistent in his acknowledgement of his own guilt. As he lies in bed on his first and only night alive on the island, he tells himself that his social ostracization was caused by a "lying rumour."[2] This is in spite of the fact that he just admitted to himself moments earlier that he deliberately sent Richmond to die. Perhaps the old habit of denial ebbs and flows. A very short time afterwards, the General admits to himself that he has felt guilt over his actions for a long while, as evidenced by his discomfort over a Bible passage where David committed exactly the same action that he had.

The General is also quite vague in terms of time. As he lies in bed, he notes that the death of Richmond occurred fifteen or sixteen years previously, though during his first appearance in the book, he seems to think that the death happened three decades earlier, nearly double the amount of time that actually passed. As the date on the record indicates, Richmond was killed twenty-two years earlier. It is possible that the General is in an early stage of some form of dementia, where he is sharp and lucid at certain times, but mentally fuzzier at others.

The last thought that readers see pass through the General's mind before he falls asleep is that he does not want to leave the island. While most of the others exhibit strong indications of the will to live after the first two deaths, the General has completely made his peace with his impending demise. The vagueness and unfinished, choppy sentences he exhibits on certain occasions may or may not be signs of the early stages of dementia. Lombard and Blore both declare that the general is "ga-ga," but this is an over-exaggeration of the condition of a man who is still capable of reasoning at a level equal to or exceeding that of his fellow guests.[3] No one else discussed the situation on the island with the General, but his declaration that none of them would leave the island alive indicates that he figured out Owen's plan on his own, and on a certain level, accepted it.

Before he dies, the General's love for his wife is reflected by his belief that Rogers could not possibly have murdered his own spouse—a faulty bit of reasoning, but it reflects the depth of Macarthur's emotion towards his marriage, as he could never have harmed Leslie. His last hours are spent in quiet reflection, looking out at the sea. When Blore approaches him and informs him of the search for someone else on the island, the General shoos him away, saying "There is so little time—so little time. I really must insist that no one disturbs me…. You don't understand—you don't understand at all. Please go away."[4]

These enigmatic words are open to multiple interpretations. Perhaps Macarthur, knowing that his remaining time on earth is quite limited, does not want to waste it chatting with Blore. Perhaps Macarthur, who regularly attends church, is trying to pray silently, cleansing his soul before passing on to his final judgment. Perhaps he just wants to luxuriate in the memories of his beloved wife. Whatever the reason, the General has decided that quiet contemplation is the best use of his remaining time.

Yet despite the General's wish not to be disturbed by Blore, he does not insist on spending his remaining hours completely alone. One of the General's last recorded conversations is with Vera, as he confesses his crime and declares that he has found peace. As he speaks, it is as if a heavy load has been removed from him, as he says, "The blessed relief when you know that you've done with it all—that you haven't got to carry the burden any longer."[5] What is this burden? It might be guilt, or perhaps loneliness, or horror at the realization of the terrible acts one is capable of committing. Perhaps a combination of all of these is possible. It is not explained why the General pushed Blore away, but happily spoke to Vera. It is possible that he preferred Vera to Blore in terms of personality, and it is also plausible that a young, attractive woman like Vera may have reminded the General of his late wife. Perhaps the General just needed time to organize his thoughts and finally examine his conscience thoroughly, and though he was not ready when Blore arrived, the General had finished his self-scrutiny once Vera arrived.

It is unknown whether or not he believed that he would be the next to die, or if he was deliberately trying to provoke the killer into murdering him next. Having read the nursery rhyme, the General could have realized that his declaration might fit the "staying there" portion, and consciously or unconsciously tried to position himself as the next victim.

When the General dies, it is from a powerful blow to the back of the head with an unknown blunt instrument. It is not stated whether the General saw or heard his assassin coming, and stoically awaited the executioner. The killer makes a note of the fact that his death was quick and painless, as those judged least culpable got easier deaths with less psychological strain. Of all the characters, it is the General who reflects upon his actions most thoroughly and takes responsibility for his actions the earliest. Arguably, this speaks well as to his moral character as compared to the others, though this might be a point of contention amongst readers. What is not in doubt is that the General was a sad and lonely man, who was fully aware that his killing a man brought him no benefits in the long run. He came to the island spiritually exhausted, and when death finally came to him, he welcomed it.

[1] Christie, *And Then There Were None*.

[2] Christie, *And Then There Were None*.

[3] Christie, *And Then There Were None.*

[4] Christie, *And Then There Were None.*

[5] Christie, *And Then There Were None.*

Chapter Six

Thomas Rogers

Technically, "the butler never does it" in an Agatha Christie novel. In one book, a criminal briefly pretends to be a butler, and in *And Then There Were None,* the butler is *a* killer, but in no novel does a genuine butler prove to be *the* central villain.[1] Most of the butlers in Christie's books are essentially background characters, the vast majority of which are simply walk-on roles. One provides a bit of comic relief by unsettling his employer with his shaky fragility, causing the lady of the house to fret over the possibility that he will smash the Christmas pudding. Another goes above and beyond the call of duty in a Bellocian decision to play the old retainer and attempts to protect his employers by polishing potential fingerprints off a weapon.

Of all the butlers in the Christie oeuvre—and there are fewer than one might expect, despite the number of mysteries set at large country houses—none would be a less welcome employee than Thomas Rogers, who deliberately allowed his employer to die in order to receive an inheritance.

At least, it is strongly implied that he and his wife are guilty. It should be noted that of all ten characters, the only two characters who do not admit what they have done, to themselves or others, are the servants. All the other characters confess their guilt verbally to themselves or others, and most characters provide at least one direct glimpse into their troubled psyches, where they confront their culpability in the confines of their own brains.

Thomas and Ethel Rogers do not confess. Mrs. Rogers is bundled off to bed immediately after the prerecorded accusation, and never says a word either way about her own culpability. Rogers, in comparison, makes a brief profession of innocence and no more. While his wife is the sole person on the island who is denied a glimpse into the workings of her mind, a couple of brief scenes are given to chart Rogers' growing agitation, though none of these musings have anything to do with accepting responsibility for the death of his employer. His primary obsession is with the smooth and orderly running of the household. One character remarked upon "the trained servant complex" in *The Murder of Roger Ackroyd* with genuine incredulity when the sight of a corpse did not prevent the butler from catching a vital clue based on a single item in the room that was out of order.[2]

"The trained servant complex" is the primary motivating factor in Rogers' mental anxiety and physical actions on the island. When his wife dies, he refuses to allow himself time to grieve (though it is quite reasonable for the reader to wonder how mournful he really is over the untimely death of Mrs. Rogers). Instead, he takes on his late wife's workload in addition to his own, and prepares the meals in addition to his other duties. When the bodies start to pile up, his primary obsession is the vanishing figurines. The disappearance of the household items is a minor factor compared to the actual murders, yet Rogers notices a missing figure when most people would have been thinking only of a recently poisoned young man and an unexpected accusation of murder. After three deaths, and all the others are grappling with the realization that one amongst them is out to kill the rest, Rogers rushes to check to see if another statuette is missing. Additionally, shortly after the guests have all realized that a killer is at work on the island, Rogers is fixated upon the disappearance of the bathroom's scarlet oilsilk curtain. Shortly before his own demise, Rogers takes more care to prevent additional figurines from disappearing than he does to protect himself. Rogers does not seem to love his job, but he allows his job to overwhelm his life. Perhaps it is a coping mechanism—focusing on the orderly running of the house allows him to distract himself from the fact that his life is in grave danger.

Notably, hardly any of the guests seem to view him as a person, only as a servant and as a potential threat. When most of the guests communicate with him, it is about household matters. After the General's death, Rogers is the only person left out of the conference. Doctor Armstrong talks to him briefly after Mrs. Rogers is found dead, and Vera has a short exchange with him when they realize that a third figurine has gone missing, but the only person on the island to converse with him regarding their threatening situation is Blore. Shortly after the third murder, the two men speak while Rogers is polishing the silver. Rogers expresses his confusion and wonders who the killer could be, and when Blore is unspecific about his suspicions, Rogers, in a state of severe agitation, declares, "I don't know. I don't know at all. And that's what's frightening the life out of me. To have no idea…"[3]

While Rogers is unquestionably in a state of severe *agitation* after the third death, he is not necessarily experiencing *guilt*. As noted earlier, Mr. and Mrs. Rogers are the only characters on the island who never expressly confirm their culpability. The possibility remains that the doctor who examined their late employer may have made a mistake in accusing them, and the only supposed proof of their guilt remains Wargrave's assertion that they are guilty based on his extensive knowledge of observing people accused of crimes. The minds and personalities of the pair might have been warped by false allegations and suspicions rather than actual guilt. Rogers, like his wife, remains somewhat of an enigma. If he is indeed guilty, then he simply sat back and allowed his employer to die, all for a small amount of money that did nothing to change his life significantly for the better. Additionally, if he was the driving force of the crime as suspected, he is also a manipulator and a bully who crushed his wife's spirit. Rogers' failure to realize that preparing the firewood placed him squarely in the killer's nursery rhyme sights illustrates at best a lack of imagination and at worst an instance of blind stupidity, or at least prioritizing domestic expectations and duties over self-preservation.

All the guests agree that Rogers was a stellar butler. At least, as long as his employer did not put him in the will…

[1] To minimize spoilers, the specific book will not be mentioned.

[2] Agatha Christie, *The Murder of Roger Ackroyd* (HarperCollins 1926, 2011 ed.), Kindle.

[3] Christie, *And Then There Were None*.

Chapter Seven

Emily Brent

More than one commentator has described Emily Brent as a dark version of Christie's legendary sleuth Miss Jane Marple. Both are older women, never married, religious, and are fond of knitting. Miss Marple takes young orphaned women into her home and trains them to be excellent domestic staff, while girls who enter service for Miss Brent are not so lucky. While Miss Marple's knowledge of human nature is essentially a trademark, Emily Brent has precious little insight into the human condition, or even her own actions. Emily Brent is passionately devoted to her personal moral code, but she fails to realize just how deeply her intense disapproval affects others.

Cold, self-righteous, and condemnatory, Miss Brent is still a complex character. In her first appearance, she looks about the other passengers in the cabin and revels in her self-superiority for handling the heat and discomfort with more supposed dignity than her fellow travelers, mentally lambasting other people for desiring anesthesia during dental procedures, or requiring sleep medications. Furthermore, she sniffs at young women who gain weight or wear revealing bathing suits at the beach. While she has no tolerance for weakness or frailty in others, she still has more accepting views on race than some of the younger characters. When Lombard and Vera both express the belief that Africans are lesser beings than white Europeans, Miss Brent sharply rebukes this bigotry, stating that people of all skin colors are brothers.

Early in the book, Miss Brent prides herself on the maintaining of her physical standards, such as perfect posture. It is, therefore, a telling irony that as the narrative progresses, she starts to lose her iron control over her own mind. At one point, she drifts off into a brief fugue and scrawls a sentence blaming her late maid for the murders in her diary. In her final moments, as she hears her killer approach her, she imagines that it is Beatrice Taylor coming for her. Clearly, she is suffering from mental strain, possibly out of fear for her life, and possibly she is finally worried about her soul.

Miss Brent also seems comfortable with traditional gender roles, as once both servants are dead, she works with Vera to take over cooking breakfast. Alternatively, she may wish to exert control over the food preparation to eliminate the possibility of someone poisoning her morning bacon and eggs. She also refuses to discuss the circumstances of her maid Beatrice Taylor's pregnancy and suicide with the group, declaring in chapter seven that it was "not a fit subject to discuss before gentlemen."[1] It was apparently perfectly proper to talk about it with Vera, as it was a matter women could speak about amongst themselves.

While Miss Brent crumbles mentally in her final hours, she feels powerful fear, but she never really feels repentance. When she confidently declares that she has always followed the dictates of her conscience, there is no evidence to indicate that she is being deliberately deceitful when she makes this statement. She genuinely believes in the righteousness of her actions, so when, in her own view, she condemned a sinner and refused to become complicit in those actions, she was upholding her high moral standards. Yet in her final moments on earth, her thoughts center on Beatrice Taylor, imagining her returning dripping wet from the river. She clearly feels fear, though it is unclear if she actually feels guilt. It is not explicitly stated if she has come to understand the damage she has done and feels remorse for how her actions led to her maid's suicide, or if she is simply panicking over the prospect of her own imminent death.

It is important to remember that Vera's amateur psychology, attributing Miss Brent's rigidity to being repressed as a child, is not necessarily an accurate cause of the elder woman's mental make-up. She was taught to be morally and physically upright from an early age, but there is no evidence to indicate abuse or emotional neglect. Her father was a colonel who possibly emphasized the importance of posture based on his military training. At the age of sixty-five, she appears to be living off of an inheritance, though the income from these funds has become much reduced in recent years, so she is forced to economize.

Miss Brent's severity is so striking that it causes several of the other guests to turn against her. Vera, Blore, and Armstrong all suspect her due to her attitude and are repulsed by it.

It is interesting that Wargrave explains that he heard about the Taylor suicide from a "memsahib" in Majorca.[2] A memsahib is a term for the wife of an English official in colonial India. Who was this woman, and how did she know about the case? Most likely, the memsahib must have been in England around the time of Taylor's death. Could she have been Beatrice Taylor's mother, or some other relative or family friend who found out about the situation too late to help? Or might she have had some connection to the baby's father? All of this must remain pure speculation, but it is an intriguing line of inquiry.

Emily Brent caused Beatrice Taylor's death through words, crushing the unfortunate girl and causing her to commit suicide. It is notable that in other works, Christie does not consider such an action to be morally equivalent to murder. In one novella, a woman with much to live for is driven to suicide through the pressure of a blackmailer. When the dead woman's friend attempts to frame the blackmailer for murder as revenge, Poirot figures out what really happened and sternly rebukes the friend, informing her that, as cruel as the blackmailer was, the act of suicide was ultimately the dead woman's own. Likewise, in another novel, when a man blames himself for roping another individual into an illegal scheme, leading to a guilt-ridden suicide, a female character informs the surviving man that he is not morally responsible for the death, as his partner in crime was an adult who was perfectly capable of choosing to decline the criminal proposition, and chose to commit suicide at his own volition.[3] Apparently, Wargrave takes a much dimmer view of provoking a suicide.

Emily Brent caused Beatrice Taylor to kill herself and her unborn baby by haranguing her and leading her to believe she had no hope for the future. Miss Brent did not intend for her maid to commit suicide, but she ought to have considered that outcome. It is a situation that has become increasingly relevant and discussed in the contemporary age of cyberbullying. Countless people denounce and attack others, often based on partial truths, lies, and misconceptions, leading to wrecked careers, damaged personal lives, and suicides. Very few people are brought to account for such actions. One wonders if the people who have driven others to despair through social media will ever be publicly accused and punished as Emily Brent was...

[1] Christie, *And Then There Were None.*

[2] Christie, *And Then There Were None.*

[3] Once again, the names of the works in question have been withheld to avoid spoilers.

Chapter Eight

Justice Lawrence Wargrave

During the early years of Christie's writing career, her first husband's employer insisted that she turn him into a character in one of her novels. According to her *Autobiography*, in her early drafting for this novel, she made him the victim. When she informed her spouse's boss of her plans, he became indignant and insisted upon being made the murderer, "Because the murderer is always the most interesting character in the book."[1]

Readers can debate over whether or not Wargrave is *And Then There Were None's* most interesting character, but he is certainly one of the most complex of Christie's villains. While most killers murder for money or romance, Wargrave is one of the very few characters to kill for justice.

The first glimpse into the true nature of Wargrave's psyche is provided in the book's conclusion:

"From my earliest youth I realized that my nature was a mass of contradictions. I have, to begin with, an incurably romantic imagination. The practice of throwing a bottle into the sea with an important document inside was one that never failed to thrill me when reading adventure stories as a child.

I was born with other traits besides my romantic fancy. I have a definite sadistic delight in seeing or causing death. I remember experiments with wasps—with various garden pests ... From an early age I knew very strongly the lust to kill.

But side by side with this went a contradictory trait—a strong sense of justice. It is abhorrent to me that an innocent person or creature should suffer or die by any act of mine. I have always felt strongly that right should prevail.

It may be understood—I think a psychologist would understand—that with my mental makeup being what it was, I adopted the law as a profession. The legal profession satisfied nearly all my instincts.

Crime and its punishment has always fascinated me. I enjoy reading every kind of detective story and thriller. I have devised for my own private amusement the most ingenious ways of carrying out a murder."[2]

In these five paragraphs, the reader is shown a heretofore unrevealed side of Wargrave. Until this point, Wargrave is shown as being consistently calm and logical. Certainly, there is no hint of an "incredibly romantic imagination."[3] His dry, precise mind stands in contrast to this, but it is possible for opposites to exist in the same brain. In many ways, Wargrave is a descendant of Robert Louis Stevenson's Dr. Jekyll and Mr. Hyde. The good personality, the principled defender of law and order and punisher of the guilty, was dominant for most of his existence, but as his life reached its close with a terminal diagnosis, the sinister half, steeped in bloodlust and sadism, demanded satiation.

Wargrave may have inspired later crime writers to create a fictional murderer who slakes his urge to kill by slaying other murderers. The television series *Murder One* (1995-1997), concluded its run with the six-episode story arc "Diary of a Serial Killer," featuring Pruitt Taylor Vince as Clifford Banks, a multiple murderer who justified his crimes by only targeting violent criminals. Vince won an Emmy for his performance.[4] Beginning with *Darkly Dreaming Dexter*, Jeff Lindsay created the character of Dexter Morgan, a blood spatter analyst who kills people who got away with murder over a series of novels. Michael C. Hall was also lauded with industry awards and nominations for playing Dexter Morgan on the television show *Dexter* and multiple spin-off series.[5]

Just as *And Then There Were None* inspired future crime writers, its conclusion also references an earlier classic mystery. When Wargrave admits to enjoying reading crime fiction, there is a subtle Easter egg to a Sherlock Holmes short story from *The Case-Book of Sherlock Holmes*, where a suicide is committed in a very similar manner to how Wargrave ends his life. It is certainly possible that in the context of Christie's novel, Wargrave read Sir Arthur Conan Doyle's work and realized that he could use this solution to his own ends. The eyeglass cord is mentioned once earlier, in chapter ten, where Wargrave plays with it. Upon knowing what it will be used for later, one can theorize that he was thinking about his plans for it.

Wargrave was one of the most skillful planners of murder in Christie's oeuvre. He spent months, possibly years working upon his crimes. None of it would have been possible if he had not been so successful in his legal career, allowing him to save up the funds necessary to bankroll his endeavor. While he is often a cold presence in the book, he must have been able to display warmth and friendliness when he wished to, as he explains how he learned about his future victims by developing a conversational gambit that led to people talking about how they knew individuals who got away with murder. People would not share such information with a man they did not wish to converse with, so Wargrave must have been able to adopt the persona of a man people would be willing to confide in, even if he was a total stranger. Again, this shows how Wargrave was more than just a man who enjoyed watching defendants squirm in court. Whether this friendlier face was a genuine aspect of his contradictory character or simply a mask he could don at will is unknown, but whatever dark tendencies were rising to the surface, he could serve as a functioning member of society. His social skills would be crucial to winning over Armstrong to be his ally.

Certainly, there was a level of luck to his master plan. All it would have taken was for one individual to catch a cold and stay home, or happen to observe him committing one of the murders, and the whole plan would have been ruined. A plan as complex as Wargrave's could have been easily derailed. No matter how much care went into precautions, the element of random chance always held the potential to send everything crashing to pieces. Perhaps it was luck, maybe it was some divine—or demonic—force supporting him, but Wargrave's plan went off without a hitch. He could have chosen to poison each target quietly, one by one, spaced out over time and place, and then no one would have suspected him of having a hand in the deaths of unrelated strangers. But Wargrave was determined to commit an unforgettable crime, a murder on a grand scale, that would live in public memory forever. What is more, he wanted to watch his victims suffer, and he wanted to play a part in it. He wanted to be the star, director, producer, and writer of the show. He knew that he was terminally ill, and he dreamed of going out in a blaze of glory.

Throughout the novel, it is apparent that Wargrave tried to exert as much control over the narrative as possible. He takes control of the investigation at every point, making sure that all the characters explain how they came to be invited to the island, and discussing the allegations against them. Though the characters of the novel accept this as the embodiment of the law settling into his old familiar role, in reality, Wargrave is acting as puppet master. He makes sure that everybody is aware of the structure of the narrative he is creating. Left to their own devices, the others could have perplexedly gone to bed, but Wargrave wanted to make sure everybody knew what was going on before the murders started, with the exception of Mrs. Rogers, who he deemed was the victim of her husband's pressure, and deserved to escape additional mental strain. Wargrave wanted all the information to come out in his own prejudged good time. When Lombard was about to reveal his suspicions about Blore (then known as Davis), Wargrave stops him, claiming the dramatic accusation for himself. Wargrave does give himself away a bit there, as most people would have been so shaken up by the allegation against them that they would not notice the absence of Davis in the accusations, or remember the full name William Henry Blore. The other characters write this off as the judge's excellent memory, when in fact, it is due to familiarity with the backgrounds of the guests.

When Anthony Marston makes note of the distinctiveness of their missing host's name, Wargrave gives a visible start. Perhaps he was worried that Anthony or someone else would realize the pun of the initials and last name. It can be theorized that Wargrave was desperate to keep the "U.N. Owen is UNKNOWN" line for himself. He possibly rehearsed it many times, took pleasure in announcing it to his future victims, and made sure to deliver it at a time when it would receive the maximum dramatic impact.

He hammered home his point with the follow-up comment that their host was "a madman—probably a dangerous homicidal lunatic."[6] No one was talking about murderous intent prior to Wargrave's intimation that this was more than a practical joke. He made sure that the other guests were put in fear for their lives as soon as possible.

Not only that, but Wargrave demonstrates petulance when someone else cuts in on one of his lines. Perhaps he had hoped to draw the ten soldier boys and the rhymes to everybody else's attention, but he waited too long. In chapter three, as dinner is wrapping up, Marston observes the ten figurines on the table, and Vera counts them and makes the connection to the rhyme framed in her bedroom. In response, "Mr. Justice Wargrave grunted, "Remarkably childish," and helped himself to port."[7] Perhaps some of this was meant to distance himself from the coming murder patterns, but it may also be sulkiness at having one of his big reveals being taken from him.

Throughout the rest of the story, Wargrave allows others to come to some conclusions themselves, such as noting the correlation of the deaths and the rhyme, and deciding to search the island. For someone who does not miss a trick, it is notable that Wargrave does not suggest murder when Armstrong states that suicide is the only explanation for Marston's poisoning. Perhaps he did not want to draw excessive attention to himself at that moment, perhaps he wanted to wait a bit more before advancing the prospect of deliberate murder, probably he did not want to put the others on their guard too soon. But throughout the story, he makes sure that no character can be excluded from suspicion, and he subtly tries to raise tensions amongst the others. When he says, "We must be very careful," he is not trying to save them or make his work harder.[8] By reminding them of the danger, he is increasing their sense of fear. Shortly before he fakes his death, he dissuades Lombard from restarting the generator, instead suggesting that they use candles for light. Candlelight did a far better job of allowing the judge to appear dead than electric lights would have.

Wargrave is frequently described as "reptilian" or compared to a tortoise. The animal comparison makes him sound a bit more sinister, but the tortoise metaphor makes him seem slow and old. Certainly, he was getting on in years, but committing the murders illustrates that he had to move relatively quickly and stealthily. He possibly was playing up his infirmity in order to distract from suspicion.

Wargrave could have created the greatest unsolved mystery of all time, but he chose to write a message in a bottle, knowing that the odds of it being recovered were infinitesimal. It was both an act of vanity—wanting recognition—but also a manifestation of his desire for justice– he partially desired the truth revealed for the truth's sake as well.

Human beings are not all one quality or another. Wargrave correctly realized that his personality was a mixed bag, and he could have fought his desire to become a multiple murderer. He twisted his desire for being an instrument of justice, leading to a bloodbath against the guilty.

[1] Agatha Christie, *Agatha Christie: An Autobiography* (HarperCollins, 1977, 2010 ed.), Kindle.

[2] Christie, *And Then There Were None.*

[3] Christie, *And Then There Were None.*

[4] "Murder One (1995-1997," *The Internet Movie Database,* accessed July 6, 2025, https://www.imdb.com/find/?q=murder%20one&ref_=hm_nv_srb_sm.

[5] "Dexter (2006-2013)," *The Internet Movie Database,* accessed July 6, 2025, https://www.imdb.com/title/tt0773262/?ref_=fn_all_ttl_1.

[6] Christie, *And Then There Were None.*

[7] Christie, *And Then There Were None.*

[8] Christie, *And Then There Were None.*

Chapter Nine

Doctor Edward Armstrong

One mistake can ruin a life. Sometimes that life belongs to the person who made the mistake, and sometimes an entirely innocent bystander is the one who has to pay the price for someone else's errors. This is the case with Dr. Armstrong. Once, he performed an operation while under the influence of alcohol, and his patient, Louisa May Clees, died because of it. By Doctor Armstrong's own admission, it was a simple operation, one which would have almost certainly been a success had he been sober.

The knowledge that Armstrong placed an innocent woman's life in mortal danger adds an extra layer of hypocrisy to his condemnation of Anthony Marston for the younger man's reckless speeding. Innumerable people die of drunken driving, and the fact that Armstrong was wielding a scalpel instead of behind the wheel when he imbibed was exactly the same thing morally— he deliberately impaired himself, and his actions led to a death. There is no mention that Marston was drunk, just reckless, but the fact remains that Armstrong and Marston were more alike than the Doctor would care to admit.

Dr. Armstrong got away with his crime because the one person who knew about it— the nurse assisting him—failed to alert the authorities. It is worth noting that the nurse who assisted Dr. Armstrong during the surgery also has a share of guilt to bear. After all, she could tell that he was intoxicated at the time of surgery. Perhaps she could have alerted someone and gotten another doctor to perform the operation. The epilogue indicates that the nurse is "violently teetotal" in the present day, and that the experience of seeing Dr. Armstrong kill a woman while drunk deeply affected her.[1] But could she have prevented it? The epilogue indicates that the death of Louisa Mary Clees happened while the nurse was still doing her training, and she may have been too scared of confronting an authority figure at the time. Yet even after Clees died on the operating table, the nurse could have reported it. It is not clear why U.N. Owen never considered the nurse's responsibility for what happened. Perhaps he granted her a level of pardon due to the circumstances and because she brought the case to his attention. The nurse was considered a subordinate to the doctor. Upon review, however, it seems as though the nurse might bear a level of responsibility on a par with Mrs. Rogers. She may not have wanted the death to happen, but she had the power to prevent it and report it afterwards, but chose not to, instead only using the story as a cautionary tale with the names removed long after the fact.

Indeed, Armstrong's actions took place nearly a decade and a half before the novel begins. Since then, he seems to have lived a perfectly respectable and successful life. He is highly successful and has built up a sterling reputation. As a man who places great importance upon his reputation, he responds with considerable anger when his expertise is questioned. This is especially understandable when he is wrongly accused, such as when Blore questions whether he might have "accidentally" given Mrs. Rogers an overdose. During Wargrave's summation explaining why all of them are equally under suspicion, Armstrong tries to shield himself with his professional reputation, only to be silenced by Wargrave's curt reminder that many doctors have gone mad in the past.

Yet all this propriety cannot silence one's conscience, and the reader is provided with insights into his crumbling psyche. He has an unsettling dream that combines the death of Ms. Clees with some of the other guests on the island, and this scene indicates that long-repressed memories are returning to the forefront of his consciousness. When the record first accuses him, he maintains a calm outer demeanor, but internally, he is wracked with guilt. As he has been able to devote himself to his profession for years, it does not seem like he has been hampered by an overactive guilty conscience. It is only when he is confronted with his crime and faces death that he snaps. By his final night on earth, he is a twitchy mass of nerves, chain-smoking cigarettes that he extinguishes shortly after lighting.

Armstrong begins the novel as an authority figure on the island, as all the guests defer to him in matters of how the others died. Yet as the novel progresses, any respect the others might have had for him by virtue of his profession is replaced with suspicion. Many people are conditioned to trust doctors and take whatever medicine they prescribe without hesitation. Once his fellow guests lose faith in his judgment, Armstrong's clout is drastically diminished, and it is fair to assume that he knows it and feels the change in treatment.

Contrary to many filmed versions of *And Then There Were None*, the Doctor Armstrong of Christie's original book is not a closet alcoholic. He immediately sobered up after causing Ms. Clees' death. There is no implication that he continued to perform surgical operations while being half in the bag. The adaptations that show him with a secret flask indicate that perhaps there are many other deaths on his conscience that slipped beneath U.N. Owen's radar. Not so in Christie's novel, where it is indicated that this was an isolated occurrence, one that left him too afraid and chastened to touch liquor before operating again.

The reader can be left wondering about just how good a doctor he really was. Wargrave's musings about how "All doctors are damned fools" reflect both his condemnation of Armstrong and his own thoughts on his terminal diagnosis.[2] As Armstrong's poor choices during his last day on earth indicate, he is not the best judge of character, and he makes various decisions and alliances based on personal prejudices and faulty reasoning. It is not unreasonable to transfer those flaws to Armstrong's medical career, and theorize that he quite possibly made some serious errors of judgment when diagnosing his patients and prescribing the most effective courses of treatment for them. It is also worth considering that Armstrong was under severe mental stress while he was on the island, and it is certainly possible that his reasoning may not have been up to par at the time.

Whether or not Armstrong was a good doctor is up for debate. The question of whether he was a good man is also fodder for a serious conversation. Armstrong's drinking took a life, but he then went on to have a highly respectable and successful career. Had he confessed to his actions when they happened, he might have lost his ability to practice medicine and likely would have served a term in prison, though it is unlikely that he would have been hanged. Do the lives that Armstrong saved as a doctor cancel out the life he took while intoxicated? Or should he not even be credited with saving multiple lives, as some of his actions indicate capability but mediocrity in his profession? He was a man who was easily influenced and fooled, and overly protective of his own reputation. If Wargrave's dismissive attitude towards him is to be weighed in the balance, it is possible that Armstrong, like many doctors, may have harmed some of his patients—if not outright precipitated their deaths—, though these casualties may have been wholly accidental, the result of sober best judgment that just happened to be ineffective.

Perhaps Armstrong was able to achieve a level of atonement for his crime by healing the sick. If so, he was able to earn a certain level of redemption that the others on the island did not. One thing is for certain. If he had confessed to operating on Ms. Clees while under the influence of alcohol, he very well could have saved a life: his own. Had he accepted the consequences of his actions, U.N. Owen would never have seen fit to have invited him to Soldier Island...

[1] Christie, *And Then There Were None*.

[2] Christie, *And Then There Were None*.

Chapter Ten

William Blore

William Blore is a corrupt police officer whose purchased lies led to the death of an innocent man. Midway through the novel, Blore admits to Lombard (and only Lombard, as Blore has no desire for the others to hear confirmation of his guilt) that at that point in his career, he was on the payroll of the Purcell gang, which ordered him to cover up their involvement in the London and Commercial bank robbery and to place the blame on James Landor, a convenient patsy.

Blore received only a moderate amount of financial compensation for his perjury, a fact that he grouses about to Lombard, carping that he ought to have pocketed substantially more cash for what he did for the Purcells. He does take some comfort in the promotion he received for how he wrapped up the case. Notably, Blore did not finish his career in the official police force. Landor died a little under eleven years before the events of *And Then There Were None*, by which point Blore is working as a private detective. It is not specified exactly when Blore left the force and went into business for himself. Possibly Blore reached the point where he received a pension and his financial situation was more secure, or possibly he left because he was discomforted by the hostility from his peers in the police force.

In the epilogue, the Assistant Commissioner of Scotland Yard, Sir Thomas Legge, makes it clear that he believes that Blore was a dishonest man. Legge suspected perjury at the time of Blore's testimony against Landor, but both he and one of his subordinates were unable to find any proof of guilt. Legge declares that, "I'm still of the opinion that there was something to find if we'd known how to set about it."[1] That little admission does not reflect well upon Scotland Yard. Legge may or may not have been Assistant Commissioner at the time of the Landor trial, but he must have had some significant and successful experience in investigation. Yet both he and the detective he assigned, who must also have been a capable man, failed to find any evidence despite their instincts telling them otherwise. It is unclear exactly why Blore was promoted, as the top brass could have used any number of excuses to deny Blore a chance of moving up the ranks. A distrusted man ought not to have been given a position of more power and influence. Yet despite the fact that Legge believed that Blore was lying, neither he nor one of his best men could find proof, and they both simply let the matter lie. It is notable that Legge speaks only of Blore's untrustworthiness, and never takes the time to reflect on the sad fate of an innocent man being thrown in jail. Perhaps Legge's institutional pride prevented him from going to an outside expert—say, Hercule Poirot—to find proof to expose Blore and vindicate Landor.

Legge was not the only one to suspect Blore's crookedness. In the conclusion, Wargrave explains that he learned about Blore's perjury through a conversation with his "professional brethren," though he does not clarify if the suspicious people were judges, lawyers, or policemen. Wargrave explains, "I took a serious view of his offence. The police, as servants of the law, must be of a high order of integrity. For their word is perforce believed by virtue of their profession."[2] Ultimately, plenty of people believed that Blore was corrupt, but they lacked not only the proof, but the will to attempt to prove a case against him.

Both on and off the island, Blore is the sort of man that others seem to take the measure of effectively. On the island, all of the others save the killer suspect him at some point, but he never fills anybody with fear. Lombard never treats him as the primary suspect until there are seemingly only three of them left, and even then, he mocks him as soon as Blore is out of sight. U.N. Owen uses Blore's fondness for food and regular routine against him, as well.

Lombard rightly deduces that Blore's Achilles' heel is his limited creative abilities. Shortly after Blore's confession, Lombard twists the knife and says, "Your lack of imagination is going to make you absolutely a sitting target. A criminal of the imagination of U.N. Owen can make rings round you any time he—or she—wants to."[3] When considering the death of Mrs. Rogers, Blore is so eager to clear his own name and whittle down the suspect list that he fails to consider other possibilities of poisoning besides the doctor overdosing her, her husband giving her a tainted cup of tea, or Miss Brent slipping something into the fainted woman's open mouth. It is notable that everybody seems to have forgotten that Mrs. Rogers was given brandy, and Wargrave carefully refrains from mentioning that fact; perhaps it might have jogged someone's memory of his handling the drink. When Blore brings Vera a brandy after she's frightened by the seaweed hanging in her room, he's enraged by the implication that he might have poisoned it, threatening to "knock [Dr. Armstrong's] ruddy block off."

Ultimately, it is fair to say that Blore simply is not a very good detective. He assumes that pretending to be from South Africa is an adequate cover story for his false persona, but fails to do the due diligence necessary to make his backstory convincing. Rather than saying as little as possible, he goes on long-winded spiels about South Africa, allowing Lombard, who actually is familiar with the region, to catch him in multiple errors. Blore misses many important clues, missing even the obvious link between the deaths and the nursery rhyme before someone else points them out to him. He misses most of the evidence that might point in the killer's direction, and allows his hunger and regular routine to lead him straight to his doom. It is not clear how successful Blore's detective agency is, but there is no reason to assume that he has a reputation for excellence.

Blore spends a lot of time trying to solve the crimes on the island, but never lands upon the correct scent. Perhaps his focus on investigating is an unconscious distraction from facing his conscience. Notably, Blore feels *distress*, but he never expresses *guilt*. During his nighttime remembrances of Landor, he is surprised by his recollection of the man's face after all this time, but there is no overwhelming sense of culpability, neither for Landor nor for his family. All Landor is to Blore is a man who just happened to be in the wrong place at the wrong time, a patsy whose sacrifice allowed him to make a little profit. Blore's primary feelings on the island were the will to survive, rather than guilt. Without the power of conscience, humans are scarcely better than animals. Vera was onto something when she declared that "we're the zoo..."[4]

[1] Christie, *And Then There Were None.*

[2] Christie, *And Then There Were None.*

[3] Christie, *And Then There Were None.*

[4] Christie, *And Then There Were None.*

Chapter Eleven

Philip Lombard

Christie's books, especially her standalone novels, often feature intelligent, courageous, and resourceful young male protagonists, who start the books down on their luck, and then, over the course of a criminal investigation, pair up with an equally admirable young woman, solve the case at considerable risk to themselves, and then conclude the novel with the promise of matrimony and a successful future. Upon beginning *And Then There Were None*, readers familiar with Christie's other books might think it reasonable to assume that Philip Lombard fits this mold. It soon becomes clear, however, that he is rotten to the core.

In his early scenes, where a flashback depicts his being recruited by Isaac Morris, Lombard's anti-Semitism is made apparent through his reactions to Morris. (Some of Lombard's bigoted comments are cut from certain editions.) Later, when he confesses the truth of U.N. Owen's allegations, he admits it without a trace of remorse, and justifies his actions with another bigoted remark that shows that he views the Black Africans as lesser beings.

Why does he make this confession when there is nothing to be gained from the truth? Given the fact that Lombard pressures other characters to tell the truth, it may be conjectured that, whatever his other character flaws, Lombard does not care for lying. Lombard's sins are all on the surface, but that does not mitigate them. He makes no hypocritical pretensions to virtue, but that does nothing to erase his vices.

Unlike many of the other characters, Lombard never feels guilt over his crimes. Unlike other characters, he never dreams or hallucinates about the nearly two dozen African men who died due to his abandonment. He does suffer from mental strain over the course of the novel, but none of this is due to wrestling with his conscience, as Vera, Armstrong, and Emily Brent do. In contrast, his anxiety is based entirely on his own survival. On a couple of occasions, he considers that he has a decent– though not certain– chance at making it off the island alive. Some of it is based on a sense of superiority, as he believes his sense of imagination is superior to Blore's, and that his flexible mind might save him. This may be self-serving, as his imagination never helps him anticipate any or the murders, or figure out what happened to his revolver, or any other aspects of U.N. Owen's plan, with one significant exception.

Lombard is the only character who suspects Wargrave in a sustained and focused manner. His suspicions, however, are not based on a logical analysis of the evidence, but instead due to an instinctive psychological profile. He asks himself, *which character would be so interested in punishing people who had escaped justice that he would set up an elaborate situation to target and kill nine other people?* The self-righteous Miss Brent and the former policeman Blore, perhaps, but in Lombard's mind, the judge Wargrave is most likely. Not only that, but Lombard deduces that all of that time on the bench may have turned Wargrave's brain and given him a God complex. Lombard is completely right, but even though he has correctly targeted the correct suspect, he is unable to transform his suspicions into proof. If Lombard's imagination was as nimble as he claimed, he could have come up with a clever trap to incriminate the judge. Lombard never makes an active attempt to mess up the murder plans or cause any disruption to U.N. Owen's goals. It seems as if he is simply steeling himself for a potential confrontation, as if he's waiting for U.N. Owen to kill off enough of the other guests so that he can narrow down the identity of the murderer and handle the threat in a physical confrontation.

Ultimately, Lombard is, and views himself to be, a man of action. Given the choice between thinking a situation through and taking a potentially less risky approach, he prefers to take the dangerous chance. He seems to prefer actions to reflection. He considers his dynamic approach to searching the island a more practical approach to Wargrave's "masterly inactivity" of sitting and thinking.[1] It is this approach that seals his ultimate fate. Had he talked to Vera for a while, between the two of them, they might have realized that Blore was almost certainly killed by a living person, and perhaps could have suspected that one of the corpses was not truly dead. But instead, he chose to pounce at Vera, and she proved to be a quicker shot than he anticipated.

Part of this is due to the fact that Lombard underestimates Vera as a woman, never believing she could overpower him or seriously considering the fact that she could steal his revolver. In this metaphorical act of emasculation, Vera is able to triumph over him by expressing concern over Armstrong's corpse and appealing to his prejudices towards female emotion. Having instilled an image of herself as too weak to be a threat in his mind, she is able to triumph through dexterity and distraction while he is counting on his physical strength.

Lombard should have seen Vera's actions coming, but he did not because he failed to take the time to think. He had the opportunity to save both himself and Vera, but he never bothered to use his mind to consider the situation, nor consider what might have happened to him if he were the only one left alive on the island.

In many ways, Lombard's professed zeal for self-preservation was his undoing because by looking out for number one, he failed to view other people as wholly human, not just as being worthy of life, but also as being potentially cleverer and more resourceful than he was. His own sense of superiority damaged him by blinding him to very real threats. In the scene where the characters are metaphorically reverting to more bestial types, Lombard's senses are supposedly heightened. On more than one other occasion, he is compared to a panther. That is an apt description of Lombard. He was a predator, but not the strongest or smartest animal in the jungle. He had the potential to survive, but because he focused his efforts on being ready to attack when danger came, rather than using his wits to preempt any threats, he doomed himself.

[1] Christie, *And Then There Were None*.

Chapter Twelve

Vera Claythorne

Depending on how familiar the reader is with Christie's other work, one might start the book with certain expectations of Vera Claythorne. Much like with Lombard, at first, Vera seems like a typical Christie heroine. For example, a contemporary of Christie's who had enjoyed her works over the first two decades of her career can easily be forgiven for assuming that Vera falls into the pattern of the spirited, courageous young woman whose ordinary existence is interrupted by being drawn into a mystery, which she solves with the assistance of a nice young man who she more often than not marries soon after the events of the novel. Looking over Christie's first twenty years of books, all of her full-length mysteries that do not feature either Poirot or Miss Marple fit this pattern. Tuppence Cowley in *The Secret Adversary*, Anne Beddingfeld in *The Man in the Brown Suit*, Virginia Revel in *The Secret of Chimneys*, Lady Eileen "Bundle" Brent in *The Seven Dials Mystery* (Bundle has a starring role in this book, after previously playing a supporting part in *The Secret of Chimneys*), Emily Trefusis in *The Sittaford Mystery*, Lady Frances Derwent in *Why Didn't They Ask Evans?*, and Bridget Conway in *Murder is Easy* all fit this pattern.

All seven of these heroines are intelligent and resourceful, and many of the Poirot novels have female characters in similar supporting roles. In every case, they are matched with a man who is their equal in virtues while simultaneously complementing them in terms of character with some opposite attributes, so the pair work quite well together as a team, and the pair usually get together at the end (with a single exception from the stated examples, where the heroine rejects the investigating partner she only likes as a friend in favor of her beloved fiancé who is falsely charged with murder). The general pattern would be followed in most of Christie's non-series novels for the rest of her life.

So for the readers in 1939, who had enjoyed all or at least most of Christie's earlier works, it is understandable that they would assume that Vera was yet another in a series of heroines. She has all of the aforementioned virtues of a Christie leading lady. The problem is that she also has a number of vices that set her apart from her predecessors.

When the reader is first introduced to Vera, she is identified as an underdog. Like most Christie heroines, aside from the titled ladies, she is poor. When she is travelling by train, she rides third class. She is a games mistress (gym teacher) in an inferior school, so it is implied that she is not paid very much, and she needs a temporary job to make ends meet over the course of the summer months. She is not expecting anything great, so the offer of a secretarial position is like kismet to her, for she thought that she might be stuck with a temporary governess position. For a woman working in the fields she does, Vera seems to be remarkably antipathetic towards children. The reader knows that her dead-end career is a disappointment to her, but that she has little chance at a better job due to having a coroner's inquest in her past. As she reflects back on the death that derailed her hiring prospects, the details are scanty, but there is no guilt in her thoughts, only a bit of relief over how well the inquest went for her.

As the perspective of the narrative shifts to Lombard's view, the reader learns that, in his estimation, Vera is a very attractive woman. Knowing that she is beautiful and downtrodden, the reader is initially disposed to be sympathetic towards Vera, though one can still wonder exactly what happened to provoke an inquest.

As the guests are ferried to the island, Vera responds to Narracott's suggestion that at least one guest stay behind, so there is more room for the others in the boat. It is a case of Vera knowing her place in the class system, as a secretary is distinctly below other guests, though once she gets to the island, she knows that a;;;; trained secretary is a bit above other domestic servants, like a butler and cook, so she can expect better accommodations and is not expected to debase herself with manual labor. When she learns about the guest list from Mrs. Rogers, Vera does a bit of quick calculation and realizes that two servants are expected to care for ten people—eight guests and the Owens—but Vera does not consider the possibility of having to do any "serving" herself. She is confident that her role as a secretary precludes her from having to scrub floors or even set the table. Vera does act with a certain level of authority, as she knows she represents her employers, while she simultaneously needs to defer to the comfort of the others.

After the record makes its accusations, Vera tells the story of Cyril's death, painting herself in the most flattering light possible. At this point, when reading the book for the first time, the reader may be inclined to believe her, though the wary Christie fan knows to maintain a healthy suspicion of every character.

It is not until midway through the book that the cracks start to show in Vera's façade, and the reader realizes that she is not the typical Christie heroine. Upon discussing Lombard's crime with Miss Brent, Vera displays an unnerving level of racism by dismissing the dead as "only natives" (a bit of a turnaround from the immediate aftermath of the record's allegations, when she professes to be shocked by Lombard leaving the men to die), and when Miss Brent rebukes her, Vera's response is to repress laughter rather than to feel shame.[1] Vera is still sufficiently insulated from her own guilt to be appalled by Miss Brent's self-described account of the harshness that drove her maid to suicide. Vera can mentally cast stones at Miss Brent while not detecting any hypocrisy in herself.

Over the course of the novel, Vera distinguishes herself as being one of the cleverest guests on the island, while also being one of the most emotionally affected individuals as well. Vera is quick to pick up the connections between the deaths and the rhyme, and her grasp of Mrs. Rogers' psyche is far more astute than Blore's. Vera is even able to come up with a solid argument for suspecting Doctor Armstrong of the crimes, and is able to shatter the alibi

Lombard believes he can provide for the doctor.

At the same time, Vera's nerves are shown to have frayed more than anybody else's, with the possible exception of the doctor. Vera bursts into hysterics at one point, needing to be slapped back into calmness, and by the time half the guests meet their demises, she is compared to a stunned little bird.

Little by little, more details are revealed about the death of young Cyril, and with each flashback, Vera's increasingly frayed nerves illustrate that perhaps she was not quite as blameless as she first asserted. It is not until two-thirds of the way through the novel that Vera's memories reveal the truth—that she did indeed encourage Cyril to swim out to his doom. It's at that point that the reader knows for certain that Vera is not a typical Christie heroine, and is, in fact, a cold-blooded villainess. It is at this point that readers ought to realize for certain that Vera will not receive a happy ending. Less astute readers will have believed that Christie was planning to pair her with Lombard at the end, but Lombard's own character flaws, so clearly enunciated in the early chapters of the book, preclude that. Some might have predicted a reunion with Hugo after Vera's vindication. In any event, once the reader knows that Vera is a child-killer, the reader familiar with the general rules of the Christieverse knows that Vera will face some sort of justice at the end, though it is not clear until the novel's penultimate scene that it is revealed whether or not she will receive her punishment inside or outside the bounds of traditional justice.

Like many of the other guests on the island, Vera is not wracked with guilt for most of the novel. It seems as though most of her mental distress and anxiety is based on her fear for her life. As the book progresses, Vera's self-preservation instincts are strong, such as when she instinctively rejects a drink offered to her in the wake of a shock. Even when her nerves are badly frayed, Vera is astute enough to suspect poison. In a similar vein, Vera considers barricading herself in her room and refusing to leave, though the self-preservation plan might have been shrewder if she had brought some tins of food to her room before turning the lock. None of the other characters are shown to consider prolonged isolation as a means of self-defense. Vera also comes up with reasons to suspect the missing Dr. Armstrong that escape Lombard and Blore, and when she and Lombard believe themselves to be the last two survivors, she exploits Lombard's underestimation of women to her advantage.

It is not until Vera's final minutes that she is finally confronted by her conscience. In the aftermath of the shooting, she is overwhelmed with relief, convinced that she is finally safe. After a few days of intense adrenaline and fear, she is finally at rest, though her relaxation leaves her vulnerable. Once Vera is sure that her life is no longer in danger, she loses her focus on self-preservation. Her mind wanders, and she even forgets the ending to the rhyme that has been haunting her thoughts for days, substituting the happier "he got married" ending mentally. Convinced that she has earned her happy ending, she even toys with the thought that somehow her beloved Hugo is waiting for her, ready to whisk her away to a joyous future together.

It is the sight of the noose dangling from the bedroom ceiling that snaps her from her pleasant musings. All at once, she realizes that what she did to Cyril was genuinely murder. That comprehension, combined with the fact that she had just shot a man to death, combined to make her decide that she deserves the ultimate punishment, and that she must carry it out herself. Psychologically speaking, Vera had a mental break caused by guilt and extended mental strain. Had she had further time to reflect, or a distraction, she might not have acted as U.N. Owen hoped. As it happened, she was mentally primed and suggestible to an attack of conscience.

Though Vera never knows it, she did not just take Cyril's life that fateful day, but she destroyed Hugo's future as well, as once he realized that the woman he loved had murdered his beloved nephew for the sake of a sizable inheritance, he recoiled from her, repulsed, and was left so devastated that he descended into alcoholism.

In the book's closing, it is implied that Vera was spared until the end because she was the worst of the guests. There is a pretty strong argument for this, though there is much to be said for bestowing this title upon Lombard as well. Vera took the life of an innocent child in her care, and it was all for nothing. Not only that, but she expresses no real contrition until her final moments, as her time on the island is devoted mainly to saving her own skin.

Vera is therefore the dark mirror image of Christie's typical heroine. She is a woman who puts her own desires and well-being above the greater good, and though she's an intelligent woman, the two men she suspects most of being U.N. Owen over the course of the book are innocent (of being the Soldier Island killer, that is). She is therefore not a skilled detective, as she catches a lot of the vital clues but fails to interpret them properly. Ultimately, Vera's great weakness is that she cannot see beyond the bent of her own mind– she could not conceive that Hugo could value his nephew over a fortune, and she twisted the clues she uncovered to fit her own theories, ignoring the many details that pointed in a different direction. Even though she is not the "central" killer of the book, Vera remains one of Christie's most developed and strongest villainesses.

[1] Christie, *And Then There Were None*.

II

PART TWO: Background Information and
Unanswered Questions

Chapter Thirteen

Predecessors

Agatha Christie's books are full of false accusations. People—often the official police, but frequently ordinary people with unfounded suspicions as well—wrongly accuse innocent people of crimes ranging from theft to murder. It is perhaps not surprising that, along the way, Agatha Christie herself has been unfairly accused of an act of malfeasance as well. Some fans of 1930s mystery films have noticed some similarities between *And Then There Were None* and two movies that were released a few years before Christie's much more famous book. While there are some very distinct similarities, not only is there no evidence that Christie was aware of either work, but also, the differences between Christie's work and the supposed sources of inspiration suggest that it is certainly possible that the points of comparison are indeed coincidences.

The Invisible Host is a 1930 novel by Gwen Bristow and Bruce Manning, which was adapted into a Broadway play by Owen Davis in the same year under the title *The 9th Guest*, and turned into a movie in 1934. In the story, eight prominent people, including an actress, a critic, a society matron, an influential political figure, a lawyer, a university president, and a former professor at that university, are called to a party at the penthouse of a tall building. When none of them admits to being the host, a recorded voice announces that they are all targeted for death, but if they outwit him, they will be allowed to live. The gate leading to freedom has been electrified, and it is impossible to jump or climb down from the penthouse. Over the course of the night, characters either fall victim to booby traps and attacks, or commit suicide, leading to an intense confrontation amongst the last three standing. In this story, not all of the characters are murderers. Several are corrupt, terrible people, but two are essentially decent folks, and they survive the night.[1]

A Study in Scarlet (1933) is a Sherlock Holmes movie where, for reasons of cheapness, the studio only bought the rights to the title and created a totally new plot. In this film, a group of characters form a sort of tontine, and one by one, the members of the group are killed, with little slips of paper containing couplets from the same nursery rhyme used in *And Then There Were None* being left near the bodies. No effort is made to make the deaths resemble the words of the rhyme. Since there were fewer than ten members involved, the first few couplets are not used, and there are more than two survivors at the end. The characters are not on an isolated island, but most of the crimes take place around London and at a country house. Other than the killer faking his own death, any other points of comparison are either minimal or common tropes. Christie was not the first person to look at the rhyme and to be inspired, but there is no reason why two people could not independently read the rhyme and realize how it could be used in a mystery story.[2]

The Internet Movie Database, an online resource where anybody can contribute, features comments on several pages arguing that Christie drew inspiration from the earlier sources. In the Internet Movie Database's Trivia section for *The Ninth Guest*, one anonymous commentator wrote:

"Though it runs just over an hour, nearly every element of the film's plot was replicated in Agatha Christie's "Ten Little Indians," including two servants engaged by an agency who follow the written instructions of their absent employer; an unseen host promising death to guests for their past misdeeds through an airwave device; a coward who offers to collude with the murderer in return for his life being spared; an isolated setting that disallows the guests from leaving; each death being executed in order of "unworthiness to live" through a missive of some kind; a thorough search of the premises that leads the characters to conclude that the killer is actually one of them; a total of ten characters of disparate ages, of which seven are male and three female; each surviving character divulging his or her guilty secret as the body count mounts; an uneasy romance between two of the characters who suspect each other despite their growing attraction; a male character managing the tension by drinking to excess, which seals his fate; a remainder of four characters, three male and one female; a sudden loss of electricity that prompts a shot in the dark, revealed to be a death once the lights go on; the two would-be lovers unraveling the solution to the mystery before they can be killed. Rather than a dining room centerpiece of China figurines, the film's characters come upon an ominous staircase of which each step is revealed to be a life-size coffin with the same amount of caskets as there are guests ("one for each of us…"). Whereas Christie kills off her victims over the course of a long weekend, the characters in this film die in the same evening, every time the clock strikes a new hour. Most strikingly, while the accusing host appears only once in the Christie version, he is an ongoing character in this version."[3]

While at first glance this seems to be a damning list of similarities, in fact, the author of this comment has made a number of errors. In fact, most points in the preceding paragraph are wrong to some extent. *The Ninth Guest* has multiple servants hired by an agency, and the underbutler only follows the head butler's spoken orders rather than written instructions. The voice of "U.N. Owen" comes from a record, not an airwave device, and it never promises death—it only accuses the ten guests of murder.

Not only that, but many of the supposed comparative scenes were not written by Christie in her novel or play, but were inserted into the 1945 film version, where she did not write the screenplay. There is no "coward who offers to collude with the murderer" in Christie's book or her play, though there is a scene in the 1945 film, borrowed for remakes, where Dr. Armstrong, temporarily suspecting the Judge, offers to help with the killings to save his own life. There are eleven living characters at the apartment at the start of the evening, plus one already dead body. No male character drinks to excess in the present-day scenes of Christie's original book or play, though Dr. Armstrong hits his flask hard in multiple adaptations, and Rogers imbibes heavily in the 1945 adaptation, the first victim gets tipsy in the 1965 adaptation, and four characters have a bacchanal in the 2015 miniseries. The servants survive at the end of *The Ninth Guest*, but they are rendered unconscious early on and are forgotten by the characters and the authors.

When one thinks about it, if Christie developed her plot independently, it stands to reason that the comparable scenes would need to be there. Much has been made over how the opening of *The Invisible Host* has the characters receiving telegrams, and *And Then There Were None* has the characters thinking about the messages that brought them to Soldier Island, but really, addressing how the characters were lured to the island is vital to the story. Furthermore, the telegrams in *The Invisible Host* are largely identical, whereas Christie hides clues in how each invitation is personalized and different. As for the search of the premises, such as the scene, it is vital to prove that there is no other person present, otherwise that possibility is always on the mind of the reader or viewer.

The Ninth Guest was released in London on April 17, 1934.[4] It is certainly possible that Christie saw the movie, but there is no evidence of it. In any case, there *is* evidence that Christie worked hard at shaping the plot of *And Then There Were None*. John Curran's literary studies *Agatha Christie's Secret Notebooks* (2011) and *Agatha Christie: Murder in the Making* (2012) study a recently rediscovered treasure trove of notebooks that Christie used for brainstorming her novels. Though there is much less available on *And Then There Were None* than there is on other works, it is clear from her notes that Christie spent a lot of time refining her ideas on the characters, their names, their background, their personalities, and even the number of people on the island.[5]

Furthermore, in her *Autobiography*, Christie wrote that she had written *And Then There Were None*:

"because it was so difficult to do that the idea had fascinated me. Ten people had to die without it becoming ridiculous or the murderer being obvious. I wrote the book after a tremendous amount of planning, and I was pleased with what I had made of it. It was clear, straightforward, baffling, and yet had a perfectly reasonable explanation; in fact it had to have an epilogue in order to explain it. It was well received and reviewed, but the person who was really pleased with it was myself, for I knew better than any critic how difficult it had been."[6]

It should also be noted that the idea of a novel containing multiple murders amongst a group was used long before the aforementioned movies. Anna Katherine Green, one of the first major female mystery writers, published the short story "The House in the Mist" in 1913. It features nine relatives who have arrived at an out-of-the-way house to hear the reading of their late, wealthy relative's will, being read by the deceased man's lawyer. The narrator is a stranger who wanders into the house in need of shelter. The lawyer tells the assembled individuals that they are set inherit a massive fortune each, but only the virtuous among them are worthy of the money. One young woman withdraws, but the other eight are desperate to receive the cash, though their greed is their downfall, and soon the number of heirs is sharply diminished.

Stanislas-André Steeman's 1931 novel *The Six Dead Men* is a Belgian story about six individuals who vow to build fortunes and share them in the near feature, but the plans are disrupted by the steady slaughtering of their number.

J.J. Connington, a British scientist and crime writer whose real name was Alfred Walter Stewart, published *The Sweepstake Murders* in 1931. When a group of nine individuals wins a massive lottery prize, with plans to split the jackpot, the members of the group start to meet sticky ends one by one, raising the amount of the survivors' shares.

Anthony Berkeley, Christie's contemporary and fellow Detection Club member, published *Panic Party* in 1934. It features a collection of people stranded on an island, who grow steadily more unhinged as violent deaths make them fear for their own survival.

The point of referencing these mysteries is to explain that plot points of characters being brought to an isolated location, and large groups of individuals being murdered one by one, had been around for a while.

Furthermore, the idea of people being murdered for their past crimes has a long history as well, including in Arthur Conan Doyle's original novel *A Study in Scarlet* (not the aforementioned movie adaptation). Christie just took some existing tropes and developed them in a different and ultimately more successful way than others did in the past.

The idea at the center of *And Then There Were None*, that is to say, trapped people being steadily killed, could have been created independently by any imaginative author. The legendary American mystery writing team Ellery Queen admitted once that they had developed a plot that was almost exactly like *And Then There Were None*, had started work upon the book, and they were forced to abandon it when Christie published her novel![7] Ironically, Bruce Manning and Gwen Bristow may have borrowed from Ellery Queen when they wrote *The Invisible Host* in 1930. In the book (not the film adaptation), characters are poisoned with tetraethyl lead, a toxin that kills quickly. Tetraethyl lead was the poison used in Ellery Queen's first published mystery novel, 1929's *The Roman Hat Mystery*, and the police doctor notes in that book that, to his knowledge, tetraethyl lead had never before been used as a murder weapon![8] Did Manning and Bristow read *The Roman Hat Mystery* and decide to use the poison at the center of its plot? It is possible, and if so, it shows how mystery writers may draw inspiration from other creative works without crossing the line into plagiarism. After all, Rian Johnson's screenplays for *Knives Out* and *Glass Onion* borrow multiple plot points from Christie stories, but there have not been any calls for Christie to receive co-author credit or have her name added to either of his Oscar nominations.

It should also be noted that Christie certainly drew inspiration from her own previous work. In many ways, Christie's 1936 Poirot novel, *Cards on the Table*, foreshadows many of the themes and plot points that would form *And Then There Were None* just three years later. In *Cards*, the sinister Mr. Shaitana invites Poirot to an unusual dinner party, with eight guests. Three sleuths, in addition to Poirot, are matched with four people who Shaitana believes have committed perfect murders. At dinner, Shaitana hints at their crimes, and while the four suspected killers are playing bridge, one of them crosses over to Shaitana's chair by the fire and stabs him. Poirot and his fellow detectives investigate not only their host's murder, but the deaths the suspects are believed to have committed in the past. Early on, Poirot suggests that Shaitana may have falsely accused one of his four guests, and the Belgian sleuth is correct. Ultimately, the guilty are all punished. Shaitana's killer murders one of the other suspects, frames that person for the death of Shaitana, and makes the death look like a suicide. Another suspect dies by accident, trying to kill someone else. Poirot traps Shaitana's real killer into a confession, and the fourth suspect proves to be completely innocent and winds up getting married and living happily ever after.[9]

Perhaps another point against any claims of Christie stealing the plot of *And Then There Were None* is that none of the aforementioned authors ever tried to sue Christie for plagiarism! It seems that other mystery writers were less trigger-happy to level accusations against Christie than some commentators are today.

[1] Gwen Bristow & Bruce Manning, *The Invisible Host* (Dean Street Press, 1930, 2021 ed.), Kindle. *The 9th Guest*, directed by Roy William Neill, Columbia Pictures, 1934, 1 hr., 5 min., DVD.

[2] *A Study in Scarlet*, directed by Edwin L. Marin, KBS Productions, 1933, 1 hr., 12 min., DVD.

[3] "The 9th Guest: Trivia," The Internet Movie Database, accessed July 3, 2025, https://www.imdb.com/title/tt0025566/trivia/?ref_=tt_ql_.

[4] "The 9th Guest: Release Info," The Internet Movie Database, accessed July 3, 2025, https://www.imdb.com/title/tt0025566/releaseinfo?ref_=tt_dt_dt.

[5] John Curran, *Agatha Christie's Secret Notebooks: Fifty Years of Mysteries in the Making* (HarperCollins, 2010), Kindle. John Curran, *Agatha Christie: Murder in the Making* (HarperCollins, 2011), Kindle.

[6] Christie, *Agatha Christie: An Autobiography*.

[7] Francis M. Nevins, Jr., *Royal Bloodline: Ellery Queen, Author and Detective* (Popular Press of Bowling Green State, 1974), 8, 63-64.

[8] Ellery Queen, *The Roman Hat Mystery* (Mysterious Press/Open Road, 1929, 2011 ed.). Kindle.

[9] Agatha Christie, *Cards on the Table* (HarperCollins, 1937, 2011 ed., Kindle.

Chapter Fourteen

The Clueing

In Wargrave's confession, he states that there are three clues that could point in his direction, which could potentially lead the police to figure out that he was the killer. First, the police knew for a fact that Seton was guilty, which meant that Wargrave was innocent of judicial misconduct. By a leap of logic, since U.N. Owen only wanted to kill murderers who got away with it, the only definitely innocent person on the island must be the murderer. Second, the "red herring" in the rhyme suggests that some sort of trickery led to Armstrong's death, and Wargrave is the only character to have been able to earn Armstrong's trust and then betray him. Thirdly, the fatal wound in the middle of Wargrave's forehead may be interpreted as the Biblical brand of Cain—the mark of a murderer.

The clues could have—but did not—lead the police in the correct direction. But there are other hints throughout the book pointing to Wargrave's guilt, some of which the police could not possibly have known, but the alert reader could have.

One point that is never spelled out in the novel is the fact that whoever set up everything at Soldier Island must have had plenty of money. The purchase of the island, the hundred guineas for Lombard's fee, and all of the other costs and fees add up to considerable costs. U.N. Owen would have to be a person of means. So, which of the characters have the money to spend on such an expensive venture? Islands with mansions are not cheap.

In the opening paragraph, we learn that Wargrave is travelling in a *first-class* carriage. Comparatively, Vera, Lombard, and Miss Brent are travelling *third*-class, and the accommodations are hot and crowded. If one had the money to do so, is it not logical that a soon-to-be multiple murderer would make sure that one spent as much of one's final days in as much comfort as possible? Lombard's memories show how he was down to his "last square meal," and Miss Brent reflects on how much less income she has now that her investments are yielding lower dividends. Vera is a schoolteacher at a far-from-prestigious establishment. None of them have enough money to buy an island, based on their own mental thoughts. Mr. and Mrs. Rogers are servants who still need to work for a living. Blore is an ex-policeman turned private investigator. They certainly are not rich enough for the job. The General's financial status is not given much detail. If he was living off a military pension, he could be ruled out, too, though the possibility of family money cannot be dismissed. Macarthur *theoretically* could have the necessary wealth, but the three who *almost certainly* have the necessary funds are the rich playboy Anthony Marston, the successful physician Dr. Armstrong, and Wargrave, who likely had a successful career as a lawyer before rising to the bench, and probably earned enough to pay for the island, especially if he made wise investments. Of course, he could have taken out loans knowing he would never pay them back, but it would have been hard to cover up these debts and take out the loans anonymously. He had no known children to support or worry about leaving an inheritance to, so his nest egg could have been considerable. Isaac Morris covered up the identity of the buyer too well for the police to track him down, but simply through logic, the police could have found the likely parties and found out whose personal finances were substantially depleted.

There is also a slight giveaway in section VII of chapter two, when Wargrave thinks to himself, "He didn't care for the girl, cold-blooded young hussy."[1] This is at a time when Wargrave has had barely any interaction with Vera. They have hardly spoken, and when she has been in his presence, she has been polite and professional. Other than an instinctive repulsion towards her, there's nothing to make Wargrave consider her "cold-blooded" or a "hussy." By the book's end, it is implied that his strong feelings against Vera are based on *what he knew about her previously from Hugo*, and it's her responsibility for Cyril's death, and her intention to inherit his fortune through marrying Hugo, that provokes this otherwise unexplained reaction.

During the conference held after Macarthur's murder, Emily Brent states where she was at the time of the murder:

"Emily Brent said:

"I took a walk with Miss Claythorne up to the top of the island. Afterwards I sat on the terrace in the sun."

The judge said:

"I don't think I noticed you there."

"No, I was round the corner of the house to the east. It was out of the wind there."" [2]

It is a subtle point that never gets explained in the book. Emily Brent sat on the east side of the house because it was sunnier and sheltered from the sea winds. Why would Wargrave spend the morning on the chillier, darker side of the house? The answer is that he wanted to be left alone. He wanted to sit in a place where he could make his way down to the General unobserved, where no one else was likely to see him leaving or returning.

The brief glimpses into the minds of the suspects also help provide some thoughtful clues. At the end of chapter eleven, the reader gets a quick look at the thoughts of the remaining six characters.

"And within? Thoughts that ran round in a circle like squirrels in a cage....

"What next? What next? Who? Which?"

"Would it work? I wonder. It's worth trying. If there's time. My God, if there's time...."

"Religious mania, that's the ticket ... Looking at her, though, you can hardly believe it ... Suppose I'm wrong...."

"It's crazy—everything's crazy. I'm going crazy. Wool disappearing—red silk curtains—it doesn't make sense. I can't get the hang of it...."

"The damned fool, he believed every word I said to him. It was easy ... I must be careful, though, very careful."

"Six of those little china figures ... only six—how many will there be by tonight?

...""[3]

Some of these six thoughts cannot be definitively attributed to one of the characters, but the signature line stating to "be careful…very careful" is clearly Wargrave. Paired with "The damned fool, he believed every word I said to him," it indicates that he has convinced one of the other men of a lie. As Lombard openly suspects him, and Blore is suspicious of everybody, it is implied that Wargrave is thinking of either Armstrong or perhaps one of the dead man, or even someone not currently on the island. Knowing the solution to the mystery, Wargrave is probably thinking of Armstrong and their plan to fake Wargrave's murder, though it is possible Wargrave is thinking of Isaac Morris and how his agent thoughtlessly accepted poison. The "It's worth trying" line is probably Armstrong, considering Wargrave's plan.

Earlier in the chapter, Blore suspects Emily Brent, citing "religious mania," so the third thought is his.[4] The first and last lines are so generic they could be going through anybody's mind. As for the fourth line, Emily Brent did briefly suspect herself of going mad when she had her brief fugue state while writing in her diary, but Vera might also have thought this, and "get the hang of it" could be a bit of foreshadowing.

The clue lies in the fact that the killer knows he personally has nothing to fear except getting caught, and that any character who fears being killed is therefore innocent. Looking over these mental thoughts can eliminate suspects and lead to a very shrewd idea of who the real criminal mastermind is.

In chapter thirteen, when only five guests remain, the reader once again gets a look into the characters' minds.

"And by now the thoughts that ran through their brains were abnormal, feverish, diseased....

"It's Armstrong … I saw him looking at me sideways just then … his eyes are mad … quite mad … Perhaps he isn't a doctor at all … That's it, of course!... He's a lunatic, escaped from some doctor's house—pretending to be a doctor … It's true … shall I tell them? … Shall I scream out? … No, it won't do to put him on his guard … Besides he can seem so sane … What time is it? … Only a quarter past

three!... Oh, God, I shall go mad myself ...Yes, it's Armstrong... He's watching me now...."

"They won't get me! I can take care of myself ... I've been in tight places before ... Where the hell is that revolver?... Who took it? ... Who's got it? ... Nobody's got it—we know that. We were all searched ... Nobody can have it ...But someone knows where it is...."

"They're going mad ... They'll all go mad ... Afraid of death ... we're all afraid of death ...I'm afraid of death ... Yes, but that doesn't stop death coming ...'The hearse is at the door, sir.' Where did I read that? The girl ... I'll watch the girl. Yes, I'll watch the girl...."

"Twenty to four ... only twenty to four ... perhaps the clock has stopped ... I don't understand—no, I don't understand ... This sort of thing can't happen ...it is happening... Why don't we wake up? Wake up—Judgment Day—no, not that! If only I could think ... My head—something's happening in my head—it's going to burst—it's going to split ... This sort of thing can't happen ... What's the time? Oh, God, it's only a quarter to four."

"I must keep my head ... I must keep my head ... If only I keep my head ... It's all perfectly clear—all worked out. But nobody must suspect. It may do the trick. It must! Which one? That's the question—which one? I think—yes, I rather think—yes—him."[5]

As Vera suspects Armstrong, and Lombard occasionally mentions being in tight places and worries about his revolver, the first two thoughts are probably theirs. The fact that in their private minds, they are concerned for their lives, exonerates them. The frenzy in the fourth quote eliminates Wargrave, meaning that the Wargrave stream of consciousness is either the third or fifth, with an edge towards the third, as he is reflecting on the mental trauma he is inflicting on the others. While the last quote, possibly Armstrong's, indicates his later confirmed suspicions of Lombard, Wargrave's presumed statement of "watch[ing] the girl" should probably not be viewed as a suspicion, but as his bet for the last target standing, and he proves to be correct.

In the penultimate chapter, where the official detectives recount the facts of the case, it is stated that the revolver was found right by the door of

Wargrave's room. The alert reader will know at once this is a discrepancy, as Vera is stated to have dropped the revolver at the top of the stairs, not far from Wargrave's room, but still some feet from where the police eventually found it.

Subtle cluing like this illustrates how Christie plays totally fair with her readers, but the hints leading in the direction of the killer are so carefully camouflaged that it is easy for the unwary reader to overlook them.

[1] Christie, *And Then There Were None*.

[2] Christie, *And Then There Were None*.

[3] Christie, *And Then There Were None*.

[4] Christie, *And Then There Were None*.

[5] Christie, *And Then There Were None*.

Chapter Fifteen

The New Administration

Late in the novel, Vera tells Lombard: "I read a story once—about two judges that came to a small American town—from the Supreme Court. They administered justice—Absolute Justice. Because—they didn't come from this world at all...."[1]

The short story Vera is referencing is by the American author Melville Davisson Post (1869-1930), "The New Administration." Post was a prolific writer from West Virginia who specialized in mystery fiction, including the perennially popular Uncle Abner short stories, which feature a righteous man who uses faith and insight to solve crimes. In this story, which does not feature Uncle Abner, an unfortunate defendant has been found guilty and is about to be sentenced, though the District Judge delays his final decision until two judges from the Supreme Court come to visit the following day, presumably because the federal government has a concern in crimes involving banking.

The details of the allegations are revealed over the course of the story. The defendant, Carter Johnson, apparently engaged in some questionable financial transactions, and his attorney argues that it was done to keep the failing Eighth National Bank solvent. It is revealed that Johnson is married and that his defense attorney, Sylvester Dickerman, will receive Johnson's home as payment if he successfully keeps him out of prison. A local businessman, Hiram Tollman, used to run the Eighth National before he became wealthy through his connections to the steel industry and opened his own bank, the Citizens' National. In order to make up the Eighth National Bank's deficit, Johnson invested money in Tollman's former concern, the Universal Steel Common. As the judge returns home, he rejects Mrs. Johnson's tearful pleas for mercy, rejecting her statement that Johnson's attempts to strengthen the bank's finances were no worse than what other respectable financiers had done to become wealthy, and that her husband simply trusted the wrong people.

The next morning, the courtroom is full, as the two guest Supreme Court judges sit beside of the District Judge, who does not look well. They explain that Johnson, as the cashier of the Eighth National Bank, misappropriated funds and falsified records. Johnson made poor investments with the bank's money in gas bonds, and when their value plunged, Johnson made additional poor investments that further imperiled the bank's finances. In order to disguise the shortfall, he used the wrong identifying bands around stacks of bills, making it appear that some packets of money contained more higher-denomination currency than they actually did. After confirming their belief in the correctness of the verdict, one judge declares, "That every man shall realize in his own person the result of his premeditated act is a condition of human affairs that we are not here to disturb."[2]

After this statement, one Supreme Court judge asks for Rutger Beekman to rise. Beekman, previously unintroduced, is the investor who accepted money from Johnson and made failed investments, consisting of $48,000 in Universal Steel Common, 48,000 shares costing one dollar apiece. A judge reveals that a man named Livingston Prichard was Beekman's secret partner, who allowed Beekman to buy the 48,000 shares when the true value of a share of Universal Steel stock was a quarter, meaning that the stock only cost $12,000. When the judge asks for an accounting of the additional $36,000, Beekman has no answer, but the judge reveals he already knows the truth, that the funds were converted into gold certificates and hidden away in a safety deposit box in a Montreal bank. The judge demands that Beekman turn over his key and sign the necessary paperwork for this money to be confiscated, along with the one hundred twenty dollars he received as a commission. As the 48,000 shares bought by Johnson have already been sold for $12,000, the recovered money means that the bank has been fully reimbursed for the missing funds.

A clearly agitated Hiram Tollman is then singled out by the judges. Tollman lied about the value of the initial investment that Johnson made, leading to a loss that needed to be made up for the bank's solvency. Tollman deliberately crafted a situation where Johnson bought bonds at an inflated value of three hundred percent of their true worth, leading to a $50,000 loss for his bank.

The five directors of the Eighth National Bank are then targeted, as well as Johnson's attorney, Sylvester Dickerman, who also handles the bank's legal affairs. The Supreme Court judges declare that they are aware of Dickerman's shady dealings and state that they are voiding the agreement that Dickerman would receive Johnson's house in exchange for representation, and instead, he will be paid only twenty-five dollars a day for his services. Apparently, Dickerman has already been paid more than that sum as a retainer, and he is ordered to refund the surplus to Johnson. Turning to the five directors, the Supreme Court judges announce that these men have been derelict in their duties, and must between them reimburse the court for costs, pay all of Johnson's legal fees, and take care of any other financial shortfalls that the Eighth National Bank faces.

The judges then inform the courtroom that Hiram Tollman taught Johnson those dishonest methods to embezzle funds from the bank, and that he himself stole bank funds and used the proceeds to fund the investments for his own fortune, repaying the amount he stole and keeping the rest. The judges order that Tollman must repay the $115,000 he retained for himself (the original profits plus interest) to the bank in one month's time.

Though the guilty verdict stands, Johnson is set free, as any additional punishment is deemed "excessive" and "abhorrent." At various points in the narrative, the Supreme Court judges note that many of the men they have ruled against "will presently be before" them, an unclear phrase with undertones of menace.

The other men targeted by the judges are humiliated and frightened, and when they learn that Beekman came to the courtroom not because of an official writ, but out of some ineffable sense that he had to report, and that a telegram to the District Judge supposedly from Washington D.C. actually came from nowhere discernible, several of the embarrassed men rush to the District Judge's house and discover his corpse, dead for at least a day. The story ends with a note of horror, as they all realize that the District Judge sat silently in court long after he had passed away (seemingly of natural causes), and that the two Supreme Court judges are supernatural figures sent by the Ultimate Authority.[3]

The parallels in themes to *And Then There Were None*, as well as the comparable occupation of the instruments of untraditional justice, are sufficiently obvious so as not to require outlining.

[1] Christie, *And Then There Were None*.

[2] Melville Davisson Post, "The New Administration, in *The Mystery at the Blue Villa* (Legare Street Press, 2022), Kindle.

[3] Post.

Chapter Sixteen

Inspiration from Grannie

In Part V of Christie's *Autobiography*, Christie recalls how in her later years, her beloved Grannie grew increasingly paranoid, believing that her servants were trying to poison her.

Christie writes:

"Little by little Grannie began to indulge in these fancies. She assured my mother that the servants were 'putting things in my food.' 'They want to get rid of me!'

'But Auntie dear, why should they want to get rid of you? They like you very much.'

'Ah, that's what you think, Clara. But—come a little nearer: they are always listening at doors, that I know. My egg yesterday—scrambled egg it was. It tasted very peculiar—metallic. I know!' she nodded her head. 'Old Mrs Wyatt, you know, she was poisoned by the butler and his wife.'

'Yes dear, but that was because she had left them a lot of money. You haven't left any of the servants any money.'

'No fear,' said Grannie. 'Anyway, Clara, in future I want a boiled egg only for my breakfast. If I have a boiled egg they can't tamper with that.' So a boiled egg Grannie had."[1]

It is possible that this memory spurred Christie's plans for Mr. and Mrs. Rogers. The idea of an elderly woman being killed by servants for the sake of a legacy is likely drawn from Grannie's worries, though it is unclear if there really was a Mrs. Wyatt who was killed for this reason, or if the incident was largely in her Grannie's imagination, and Christie's mother was tired of reassuring Grannie that the crime had not actually happened.

Christie used Grannie's finding safety in boiled eggs in her Miss Marple story "Strange Jest." Miss Marple reminisces about her eccentric Uncle Henry, saying:

"He was a suspicious man, too. Always was convinced the servants were robbing him. And sometimes, of course, they were, but not always. It grew upon him, poor man. Towards the end he suspected them of tampering with his food, and finally refused to eat anything but boiled eggs! Said nobody could tamper with the inside of a boiled egg. "[2]

[1] Christie, *Agatha Christie: An Autobiography*. Christie's grandmother, Margaret Miller, was nicknamed "Auntie-Grannie" because she was not only the stepmother of Agatha's father, but the aunt and adoptive parent of Agatha's mother as well. Apparently Agatha switched back and forth referring to her as "Auntie" and "Grannie" and "Auntie-Grannie."

[2] Agatha Christie, *Miss Marple: The Complete Short Stories* (HarperCollins, 1985, 2011 ed.), Kindle.

Chapter Seventeen

Burgh Island

Agatha Christie fictionalized several real-world locations in her books. Soldier Island is inspired by Burgh Island off the coast of Devon. It is a small private island, but it is a popular tourist attraction, featuring the Burgh Island Hotel, as well as residences, ruined religious buildings such as a monastery and a chapel, remnants of ancient civilizations, walking paths, and the Pilchard Inn pub. These intriguing locations inspired venues in the computer game adaptation of *And Then There Were None*.

The official Burgh Island website declares that:

Nestled on an island off the rugged Devonshire coast, 15 miles from Dartmoor National Park and the river Dart, Burgh Island is one of the best South Devon hotels. With a range of boutique rooms—each with free wi-fi and a private bathroom—a stay at our luxury hotel is a truly unforgettable experience. Surrounded on all sides by sea views, the island hotel offers stunning amenities, an award-winning restaurant and unparalleled Art Deco hotel luxury with individually designed rooms. The perfect location for a coastal wedding setting, for parties by the sea or for delightful fine dining, Burgh Island is a luxury South Devon hotel like no other.[1]

At low tide, visitors can walk to the island, but when the water rises, a vehicle called the sea tractor is generally used, though small boats are also a potential means of transportation.

Christie was so inspired by Burgh Island that she fictionalized the locale again for her novel *Evil Under the Sun* two years later, when Poirot investigates a crime at a seaside resort. She is believed to have worked on some of her novels there at a beach house, and the island was a filming location for the David Suchet adaptation of *Evil Under the Sun* and the Joan Hickson version of *Nemesis*.[2]

Constructed in 1929, The Burgh Island Hotel is decorated in the Art Deco style, though it has been remodeled and added to over the decades. Occasionally, the hotel hosts murder mystery weekends. No actual murders are known to have been committed on the island.

[1] "Burgh Island Hotel," accessed July 3, 2025, https://www.burghisland.com.

[2] Jonathan Morris, "Agatha Christie inspiration Burgh Island for sale at £15m," May 10 2023, https://www.bbc.com/news/uk-england-devon-65542868.

Chapter Eighteen

Is There More To The Death of Arthur Richmond In *And Then There Were None* Than Was Previously Suspected?

In *And Then There Were None*, all of the major characters are responsible for the death of at least one person, which is why they are summoned to a mysterious island off the coast of Devon to be punished at the hand of an unknown executioner. General John Macarthur's crime is that he knowingly and deliberately sent Arthur Richmond to his death in battle. Richmond was an officer serving under him who was having a secret affair with the General's wife Leslie. Macarthur first found out about their adulterous relationship in the following manner:

"It had come about exactly in the way things happened in books. The letter in the wrong envelope. She'd been writing to them both and she'd put her letter to Richmond in the envelope addressed to her husband. Even now, all these years after, he could feel the shock of it– the pain..."[1]

It seems that the General learned the truth thanks to a fatally stupid mistake on Leslie's part. She wrote two letters and mixed up their envelopes. That explains how the General found out about the affair, but if it was all just an innocent mix-up, then should not Richmond have received the letter meant for the General, thereby leading Richmond to realize that the General knew about the two of them? That would have happened if the letters were indeed mixed up, but according to the General's memories, this was not the case:

"He'd managed to carry on as usual—to show nothing. He'd tried to make his manner to Richmond just the same.

Had he succeeded? He thought so. Richmond hadn't suspected. Inequalities of temper were easily accounted for out there, where men's nerves were continually snapping under the strain."[2]

So if the General's observations are accurate—and there is no reason to suppose that they are not, since Richmond's unease ought to have been easily detectable if Richmond had reason to assume that his superior officer knew about the affair—then Richmond did not believe the General knew the truth, which means that Richmond did not receive the letter that was meant for the General.

If Richmond never received the letter Leslie intended for the General, what happened? Did it get lost in the mail? That is possible, but unlikely, since the if both letters were sent at the same time and the General received his, then it is improbable, and indeed, an odd coincidence, that the letter in question was lost. Could someone have stolen the letter? Possibly, but why would anyone do that? No one else that we know of had any reason to wish Richmond dead. There remains one possibility, but it is by far the most likely one. There never was a second letter. There was no mix-up. Leslie only wrote the one letter. She wrote a love letter to Richmond and sent it to her husband.

Could it have been an accident? Possibly. Leslie might have written the letter and then absent-mindedly addressed the envelope to her husband instead of her lover (her husband's last name and her lover's first name being so similar, it might have been easy to have had a mental lapse), and then mailed it without noticing the error. Yet there is another, much more sinister possibility. Leslie might have deliberately and with malice aforethought sent that letter to her husband. Why? Could Richmond have broken off the affair? Could Leslie have discovered that he was seeing another woman? And if something happened to fill Leslie with murderous rage, could she have decided to get her revenge by pretending to accidentally send her husband a letter regarding the affair?

This would have served a dual purpose. Leslie might have taken a perverse pleasure in informing the much older man she may have come to resent that she was cheating on him, and furthermore, Leslie would have known that her husband would have sought revenge. Maybe this was a particularly hurtful way of getting her husband to let her out of the marriage, but it's possible that she may not have really been in love with Richmond and simply wanted her freedom without new entanglements. Possibly she hoped that the General would kill Richmond in a fit of rage and then be executed for the crime, thereby freeing her from both her husband and her lover. And if so, the scheme went partly according to plan. The General did kill Richmond, but in a way that no one could possibly prove was deliberate. If Leslie did purposefully send her husband the fatal letter, it is possible that she may have been devastated by remorse when she heard that Richmond was dead, or possibly this may have been tempered by unease by her husband remaining alive and unsuspected. The General never suspected that the letter was sent to him deliberately, but he may have mistaken Leslie's guilt for grief. The General remembered that:

"Leslie hadn't known. Leslie had wept for her lover (he supposed) but her weeping was over by the time he'd come back to England. He'd never told her that he'd found her out. They'd gone on together– only, somehow, she hadn't seemed very real any more. And then, three or four years later she'd got double pneumonia and died."[3]

Or perhaps the *general* was Leslie's intended target. Perhaps she deliberately sent him a letter to her lover, hoping that her husband would be so devastated he would commit suicide, or perhaps place himself in mortal danger? And then, when her lover died and her husband lived, could Leslie have been crushed by her plans backfiring?

Could Leslie's guilt have been a factor in her death? Could her culpability over her affair and her crime have altered her personality, causing her to no longer seem "very real?" Very possibly. Indeed, can we be certain that Leslie's death was due solely to pneumonia and not, perhaps, an overdose of some drug? A careless physician might attribute the death to illness, or possibly oversensitivity to the widower's feelings might have caused a doctor to hush up any hint of suicide. If this was indeed the case, then the General's observations about his wife's emotional and mental decline, as expressed to Vera Claythorne, take on a very different interpretation:

"I don't know. I—don't know. It was all different, you see. I don't know if Leslie ever guessed…I don't think so. But, you see, I didn't know about her any more. She'd gone far away where I couldn't reach her. And then she died—and I was alone…'"[4]

Does any of this mitigate the General's culpability? Certainly not. The General knew exactly what we he was doing when he sent Richmond to a certain and avoidable death. The General is still responsible for abusing his authority and causing the demise of one of his subordinates. All this means is that Richmond had two people involved in his killing instead of one. Of course, the accident theory is still a possibility, and Leslie might be guilty of nothing more than a fatal blunder (aside from the adultery). It is impossible to tell for sure. The one person from the novel who could answer that question died long before any of the ten central characters in *And Then There Were None* met their fates, and Agatha Christie left no clear clues as to the truth of the matter.

[1] Christie, *And Then There Were None.*

[2] Christie, *And Then There Were None.*

[3] Christie, *And Then There Were None.*

[4] Christie, *And Then There Were None.*

III

PART THREE: Stage Adaptations

Chapter Nineteen

Christie's Stage Adaptation

Two decades into a wildly successful career as a novelist, Christie pursued her interests in another creative medium: playwriting. She had already met with some success in 1930 with her original Poirot play *Black Coffee*, but other attempts, such as her adaptation of *The Secret of Chimneys*, with the title simplified to *Chimneys*, failed to get produced, and languished in archives for decades before being rediscovered, staged, and published in the twenty-first century.

Nearly thirteen years after *Black Coffee's* opening, Christie decided to adapt *And Then There Were None* for the stage, writing in her *Autobiography:*

"I thought to myself it would be exciting to see if I could make it into a play. At first sight that seemed impossible, because no one would be left to tell the tale, so I would have to alter it to a certain extent. It seemed to me that I could make a perfectly good play of it by one modification of the original story. I must make two of the characters innocent, to be reunited at the end and come safe out of the ordeal. This would not be contrary to the spirit of the original nursery rhyme, since there is one version of 'Ten Little [Soldier] Boys' which ends: 'He got married and then there were none.'

"I wrote the play. It did not get much encouragement. 'Impossible to produce' was the verdict. Charles Cochran, however, took an enormous fancy to it. He did his utmost to get it produced, but unfortunately could not persuade his backers to agree with him. They said all the usual things—that it was unproduceable and

unplayable, people would only laugh at it, there would be no tension. Cochran said firmly that he disagreed with them—but there it was.

'I hope you have better luck some time with it,' he said, 'because I would like to see that play on.'

In due course I got my chance. The person who was keen on it was Bertie Mayer, who had originally put on Alibi *with Charles Laughton. Irene Henschell produced the play, and did so remarkably well, I thought. I was interested to see her methods of production, because they were so different from Gerald Du Maurier's. To begin with, she appeared to my inexperienced eye to be fumbling, as though unsure of herself, but as I saw her technique develop I realised how sound it was. At first she, as it were, felt her way about the stage,* <u>seeing</u> *the thing, not hearing it; seeing the movements and the lighting, how the whole thing would look. Then, almost as an afterthought, she concentrated on the actual script. It was effective, and very impressive. The tension built up well, and her lighting, with three baby spots, of one scene when they are all sitting with candles burning as the lights have failed, worked wonderfully well.*

With the play also well acted, you could feel the tension growing up, the fear and distrust that rises between one person and another; and the deaths were so contrived that never, when I have seen it, has there been any suggestion of laughter or of the whole thing being too ridiculously thrillerish. I don't say it is the play or book of mine I like best, or even that I think it is my best, but I do think in some ways that it is a better piece of craftsmanship than anything else I have written. I suppose it was Ten Little [Soldiers] *that set me on the path of being a playwright as well as a writer of books. It was then I decided that in future no one was going to adapt my books except myself: I would choose what books should be adapted, and only those books that were suitable for adapting."*[1]

Christie made a number of changes to the plot. For the purposes of staging, all of the action takes place in the living room. Some of the characterization has been expanded or enhanced. Mr. and Mrs. Rogers are given a bit more dialogue together at the beginning, and they express contempt for Blore due to his unrefined manners and cheap underwear. The General received a pair of modifications, the first being to his name. As the real-life American General Douglas MacArthur (the second "A" in his last name was capitalized, unlike the fictional character) had become a well-known figure since the book's publication, Christie altered the General's last name to Mackenzie. The General's manner of death is also changed. Instead of being bludgeoned with an unnamed blunt instrument, he is stabbed in the back with a knife.

The most significant alteration is the last five minutes. As the play was being performed in middle of WWII, Christie decided that the original ending was much too bleak for an audience who needed distractions and cheering up more than anything else, so a happy ending with a bit of romance was inserted as a means of lightening the play's final moments. In the revised ending, both Vera and Lombard survive and are actually innocent. Lombard explains he in fact tried to save the men under his command, but failed. He then decided to make a false confession after the accusatory record just to see the reactions of the others. Vera declares that it was her boyfriend Hugo who told Cyril he could go out for a swim, and that she genuinely tried to reach the child in time but failed. Afterwards, she severed ties with Hugo. Neither Vera or Lombard is convinced by the other's profession of innocence at first, and after faking a swoon, Vera wrests the gun away from Lombard. She fires, and he falls.

Immediately afterwards, Wargrave enters, delighted with the success of his plans. While Wargrave was always calm, collected, and logical in the book, in the play, Wargrave's character is clearly insane, in stark contrast to his earlier demeanor. After explaining his actions, he attempts to force Vera to hang herself, but she pleads innocence, and eventually convinces Wargrave, who still insists that she must be hanged to complete the rhyme. This is in stark contrast to the book, where Wargrave was adamant that all of his victims had to be guilty and therefore deserve his special brand of justice. In the play, guilt or innocence matters less to Wargrave than getting the desired number of dead bodies. Vera is saved by a not-dead-after-all Lombard, who picks up the dropped revolver and fatally wounds Wargrave. After remarking that women cannot shoot straight—or at least not straight enough—Lombard notes the alternative ending to the rhyme: *He got married, and then there were none.* Lombard changes the pronoun to "we," and when they kiss to the sound of the boat approaching the island, it is implied that

Lombard and Vera are indeed both innocent of murder, and that they will be able to convince the authorities that Wargrave killed the seven others, that Lombard shot the judge in self-defense, and they will be allowed to live happily ever after together.[2]

An official alternate ending to the play, based on the book's closing, was commissioned in 2015 and is now a licensed possibility for production companies who believe that their audiences will have no problem with the darker conclusion.

In an introduction to this new ending, Christie's grandson Mathew Prichard, writes:

"My grandmother's play has been performed successfully all over the world since its première in 1943 with an ending which is unique to the play and is not that of the novel on which it is based. There is much evidence that this was not her initial intention but was instead the result of what was perceived to be the needs of audiences at a very dark time in history. My grandmother never shied from taking notice of others' input and the success then and since of the play vindicates her approach and their views.

In recent years enterprising producers presenting to, perhaps, more inquiring audiences have experimented with incorporating the novel's ending in the play. This, too, has been well received leading to a controversy as to which is the "real" ending. I have no intention of settling this controversy. Instead, on the 125th anniversary of my grandmother's birth, I wish to make the choice available to all producers and directors to express their view as to the writer's intention by enabling them to choose from the 1943 (play) ending and the 1939 (novel) ending.

Drawing on papers and correspondence at the time of production and on archive material, I have commissioned a dramatic version of the novel's close. Both dramatic endings begin their unraveling with Lombard's line to Vera: "You— young, lovely, and quite, quite mad." After that, readers, producers and directors face the same choice that my grandmother faced."[3]

Should the alternative ending be used, it also makes sense to delete Lombard's lines spoken shortly before he describes Vera as, "You—young, lovely, and quite, quite mad," where he retracts his previous confession and proclaims his innocence, as this will remove any ambiguity about his guilt, thereby removing the implication that an innocent man has just been shot.

The "1939 ending" uses essentially the same dialogue between Wargrave and Vera as there is in the original 1943 play's version, until shortly after Wargrave declares, "I'm mad, but you're not." After Vera declares, "You'll never get away with it!" Wargrave explains how he will preserve the fingerprints Vera just left on the revolver, and then use the elastic cord on his eyeglasses to commit suicide and send the gun flying away. Vera professes her innocence, and then Wargrave recounts his conversation with Hugo, taken nearly verbatim from the book. Vera keeps denying her guilt, but Wargrave explains that he watched her face during the record playing, and he is certain of her culpability. Forcing her to look at Lombard's genuinely dead body and hammering home the fact that she has just killed a man, a traumatized Vera takes the last china soldier boy Wargrave offers, climbs up on the chair Wargrave has set up, sticks her head into the noose, and kicks away the chair. Wargrave moves the chair, takes the revolver, and exits. Just as a gunshot is heard offstage, the china soldier boy slips from Vera's dying hands and smashes on the ground.[4]

Theater companies have been making unauthorized changes to the stage version of *And Then There Were None* for many years. Often, in a desire to provide an additional role for a woman, at least one male part, frequently Dr. Armstrong, is played by a female, with the only significant change to the dialogue being altering the first name of the doctor during the record-playing scene. Sometimes Wargrave is given a cane and a heavy limp, or even a wheelchair, in order to play up his frailty, only to shock the audience when he comes back from the dead and reveals that he has no need for the assistance. Deviating far further from Christie's original intentions, some productions have even changed the identity of the killer, with Miss Brent and Blore being popular alternative killers, but there are reports on the Internet site TVTropes.org of Rogers, Mrs. Rogers, and even Fred Narracott being cast in the role of U.N. Owen. None of these alterations have been made with the official permission of the Agatha Christie estate. The shock value of the change is of dubious value. As the computer game illustrates, it can work thematically to cast Miss Brent in the role of righteous avenger, but given his characterization in the play, Blore as Owen is less convincing, and the timid Mrs. Rogers and the blink-and-you'll-miss-him Fred Narracott are even less effective (it is unclear why the doctor would pronounce some of these supposed victims dead or how Narracott managed to successfully hide himself on the island), and the central payoff of shifting the blame to Rogers comes with having the butler do it. Still, given the themes, the cluing, and everything else, even with the broadest possible mindset, it is hard to argue anything other than the fact that Christie picked the right killer herself, and that any attempt to mess around with her solution is to mar the play.[5]

There are a few issues with Christie's play that could use adjustment. The rhyme is never read out in its entirety, so playgoers unfamiliar with the story may not be able to anticipate the murders. This problem can be solved by making the framed copy of the rhyme over the fireplace large enough for the audience to read, or by prominently including the rhyme in the program, or even adding a voice-over to the start of the play that reads out the poem. Another issue is Blore's death. In the book, the marble clock shaped like a bear is introduced early on, and the savvy reader can predict that it will play a role in the eighth victim's murder. In the play, the bear clock is not mentioned until right after it crushes Blore. A previous reference to it, or possibly even having the clock appear onstage (Rogers could be polishing it in his opening scene and carry it away afterwards), might foreshadow its use as a weapon later.

One of the trickiest parts of performing the play is carrying out the action realistically without actually spoiling the solution. For example, the initial poisonings take place on-stage, but the observant audience member might see the killer slipping poison into Marston and Mrs. Rogers' drinks. Some productions have the killer do nothing (which in a way is a cheat, as the eagle-eyed viewer might note that the killer was on the opposite end of the stage at all times), and others have the killer actually commit the poisonings, sometimes with a hand quickly passing over a glass, or through the use of a poison ring or little vial carefully concealed in a fist. It is a dead giveaway if spotted, but if the killer is sufficiently dexterous, and if the audience is distracted by something else at the other end of the stage, it is likely that only people familiar with the story who keep a close eye on the killer will notice anything amiss. The breaking of the figurines is more challenging, as a potential smashing noise is more likely to draw attention than powder or liquid or pellets noiselessly being slipped into an inch or two of liquid. Figuring out how to arrange the breaking is a much more difficult task for the production. Some productions have the General sitting in plain view shortly before his death; others have him completely off-stage. It is a clever piece of misdirection to have all or at least several of the characters approach the General as they pass by or speak to him, implying that any one of them could have used the opportunity to stab him.

A UK tour of the play, beginning in 2023, made one major casting change. Rogers is removed, and is replaced by Georgina Rogers, a female butler. Mrs. Rogers is replaced by a housekeeper named Jane Pinchbeck (a wholly original name created for this tour), and a quick kiss indicates that the pair are in a lesbian relationship.[6]

And Then There Were None continues to be one of Christie's most popular plays and is performed regularly around the world.

The original London production was at the St. James's Theatre, and opened on November 17, 1943. Irene Hentschel directed, and Clifford Pember created the set design. The cast was as follows:

Rogers: William Murray

Mrs. Rogers: Hilda Bruce-Potter

Fred Narracott: Reginald Barlow

Vera Claythorne: Linden Travers

Philip Lombard: Terence De Marney

Anthony Marston: Michael Bake

William Blore: Percy Walsh

General Mackenzie: Eric Cowley

Emily Brent: Henrietta Watson

Sir Lawrence Wargrave: Allan Jeayes

Dr. Armstrong: Gwyn Nicholls

The New York City production debuted at the Broadhurst Theatre on June 27, 1944. It moved to the Plymouth Theatre on January 6, 1945, completing the run on June 30, 1945. Albert de Courville directed, and Howard Bay was the set designer. The cast featured:

Rogers: Neil Fitzgerald
Mrs. Rogers: Georgia Harvey
Fred Narracott: Patrick O'Connor
Vera Claythorne: Claudia Morgan
Philip Lombard: Michael Whalen
Anthony Marston: Anthony Kemble Cooper
William Blore: James Patrick O'Malley
General Mackenzie: Nicholas Joy
Emily Brent: Estelle Winwood
Sir Lawrence Wargrave: Halliwell Hobbes
Dr. Armstrong: Harry Worth[7]

[1] Christie, *An Autobiography*.

[2] Agatha Christie, *And Then There Were None* (play), in *The Mousetrap and Other Plays* (Harper Collins, 2012), Kindle.

[3] Agatha Christie, *And Then There Were None* (play) (Samuel French, 1943, 2015 ed.), 7.

[4] Agatha Christie, *And Then There Were None* (play) (Samuel French, 1943, 2015 ed.), 101-106.

[5] "And Then There Were None," TvTropes.org, accessed July 4, 2025, https://tvtropes.org/pmwiki/pmwiki.php/Literature/AndThenThereWere None.

[6] Paul Rhodes, "REVIEW: Paul Rhodes's verdict on Agatha Christie's And Then There Were None, Grand Opera House, York ****," CHARLESHUTCH-PRESS, November 23, 2023, https://charleshutchpress.co.uk/review-paul-rhodess-verdict-on-agatha-christies-and-then-there-were-none-grand-op

era-house-york/.

[7] Christie, "And Then There Were None (play)."

Chapter Twenty

Christie in a Concentration Camp

In 1947, Agatha Christie received a letter from The Hague informing her of a stage adaptation of *And Then There Were None* that she had never heard of previously. The letter was written by G.W. Fris, a Dutch former prisoner of war who told her how *And Then There Were None* had helped him and his colleagues keep their hope and their sanity while being trapped in the Nazi concentration camp Buchenwald, located in central Germany.

The following is the letter Fris sent to Christie, unabridged and unedited save for correcting minor typographical errors, altering the title of the play to *And Then There Were None,* and removing the addresses of the sender and the recipient. Fris's English is good but not perfect, so there are a few mistakes of tense and phrasing that may catch certain people's attention.

> The Hague, April 23rd, 1947
>
> Dear Mrs. Christie,
>
> Being an officer of the Dutch administration in the Netherlands—East—Indies—on the moment of the German invasion into the Netherlands on furlough in our country—I have been interned by the Germans during their occupation of our country. Together with my fellow-prisoners we have been hostages for the German citizens who were interned on the basis of the international laws by

the Netherlands–Indies authorities on the moment of the German invasion into the Netherlands, and we even remained in prison during the Japanese occupation of the Netherlands–Indies.

For more than four years we have been interned behind the barbed wire fences in the concentration camp of Buchenwald and in four more camps in Holland.

With several fellow-prisoners we have done everything to keep the morale of the hostages as high as possible and to bring them some entertainment, camp-life being very dull indeed. So we organized a series of performances on the stage, primitive as it may have been, played by amateurs of course, and the play also written by an amateur-dramaturg.

For one of our troubles was that we could not obtain the right play which fitted in our possibilities and our circumstances, therefore I have to write the plays myself– an entirely new job to me.

Once I got your splendid thriller *And Then There Were None* into my hands, smuggled into our camp from the other side of the barbed wire fence, and it gave me the idea of writing a play in three acts based upon this novel. Our performance was a great success thanks to the very clever and perfect plot of your novel.

At present I am working at the Colonial Office at The Hague (Ministry for the Overseas Territories of the Kingdom to be exact) and for some weeks the pre-war entertainment-club of this office has been reestablished after having been lifeless during the German occupation.

The committee wanted to organize a party for celebrating the revival of the club, consisting of a play and dance afterwards. Knowing about the performance of the *And Then There Were None* under such strange circumstances played and written by hostages in a German camp, the prisoners belonging to the Netherlands–Indies administration which affairs in Holland are administered by the members of this club, the committee egged me to stage my play once again, now in full freedom.

I agreed, the performance was fixed on May 20th and the rehearsals started. I never thought about the copy-right, our party being strictly reserved for members of the club and their guests, no charging for admission and the press not being invited.

Today I am informed about the existence of an authorized stage-version of your novel. It is too late by now for stopping our rehearsals the theatre already being reserved for our party and on the other side our very young club not being able to pay the rights.

Under these circumstances I am applying to the author of the *And Then There Were None* for begging her special permission for our above mentioned performance without any troubles about the rights of translations, staging, etc. If you would be so extremely kind as to give your consent you are helping a young club without inconvenience for others and our memories of our camp-days will be much brighter. We would be very grateful indeed if you would comply with our request.

Yours faithfully,

G.W. Fris[1]

This little-discussed event gives us a fascinating look into not just one of the darkest aspects of twentieth-century history, but it also provides terrific insight into Christie's enduring appeal and how the strong moral themes of her works resonate with readers.

The Dutch East Indies were a collection of colonies located across what is currently known as Indonesia. It is not clear exactly what position Fris held in the colonial government, but it was probably prominent enough to warrant the Nazis' arresting him in order to drain the Netherlands of its leadership, so as to better control the country during the occupation.

The Nazi invasion of the Netherlands began on May 10th, 1940, and the nation's primary defense forces fell four days later, though battles in certain areas would continue for a few more days.

The verb tenses Fris uses are a bit confusing. Upon first reading, it sounds as if he was back home in the Netherlands at the time of the Nazi invasion, and was arrested soon afterwards and imprisoned. When he mentions the "Japanese occupation of the Netherlands-Indies," a casual reading of the end of the first paragraph makes it sound as if he might have been transferred to a camp in present-day Indonesia, though it does seem unlikely though not impossible that the Nazis would ship prisoners of war halfway around the world. The confusion of the last sentence is probably due to Fris's fluency in English.

Fris states that he was held in prison for over four years, indicating that he was released after the fall of the Nazis in the spring of 1944. He mentions being held in "Buchenwald and in four more camps in Holland." It is possible that he is not describing his experiences in order, and was originally held in Dutch camps and then moved to Buchenwald. It was not unusual for prisoners of war to be moved around for various reasons, such as security or to dissuade Allied bombings of certain areas for fear of killing Allied P.O.W.'s. It is not known precisely when his internment at Buchenwald began and ended. It is necessary to provide some information on the nightmarish conditions at Buchenwald in order to provide a glimpse into what it meant to be imprisoned there.

The Buchenwald concentration camp was built in 1937. It had a very wide-ranging population of prisoners, including Jewish people; migrating ethnic groups such as the Roma and the Sinti; people who were labelled "work-shy" such as the homeless; members of the clergy, especially Catholic priests who preached against Nazism, political activists from certain Socialist or Communist groups who were deemed particular threats to the Nazi regime, Freemasons, currently-held prisoners and recently-released convicts; the mentally ill; the physically disabled; prisoners of war from across Europe, particularly Eastern Europe; and other unfortunate people who fell victim to the Nazi desire to rid their society of people they branded inferior or dangerous. Approximately 238,980 people were imprisoned at Buchenwald over the course of the Second World War. 53,926 of them died, or about twenty-two percent of the total prisoners.[2] The vast majority of the prisoners were men, with fewer than a thousand of the captives being female. Some of the earliest female prisoners were forced into a brothel at Buchenwald and sexually exploited by guards, but most of Buchenwald's female prisoners were jailed during the last year or so of the war.

Buchenwald was technically a "concentration camp," not a "death camp," which meant that the internees were not immediately marked for slaughter. Prisoners were generally not tattooed with identification numbers in non-official "death" camps, but just because the prisoners were supposed to be imprisoned and left to live inside the camp rather than murdered in gas chambers and in other horrible manners, that did not mean that life expectancy was high. Poor food and minuscule portions led to all sorts of health issues; and awful sanitary conditions, close quarters, and wretched medical care led to outbreaks of various diseases such as consumption. Many prisoners were forced to toil until they dropped, chopping down trees and performing other forms of harsh manual labor until they were literally worked to death. Twisted "science" experiments were performed on many inmates, who were injected with various chemicals and diseases, operated upon, and otherwise mutilated.[3]

Furthermore, many guards and camp officials murdered inmates as they pleased. Some were simply shot and died swiftly, being spared extended suffering. Others were not so lucky. One infamous sadist, Walter Sommer, was dubbed "The Hangman of Buchenwald," due to his habit of torturing inmates by hanging them by their wrists upon trees, and the howls of agony led to the woods being dubbed "the singing forest." The fates of two Catholic priests, Mathias Spannlang and Otto Neururer, are debated, as some commentators say they were crucified upside-down at Sommer's orders, while other researchers say they were hanged, and other reports suggest deaths by beating or medical experimentation.

Two of Buchenwald's most sadistic officials were the married couple Karl-Otto and Ilse Koch. Karl-Otto was placed in charge of Buchenwald for most of the first four years of its existence. During his first year there, he married Ilse, who was working as a guard. Many women worked as guards at predominantly male camps. The two soon developed a reputation for extreme cruelty. Under the Koch's tenure, prisoners were routinely robbed and tortured, allegedly being beaten, physically and sexually assaulted, and mutilated. Ilse had a reputation for profligacy, and rumors abounded of her having affairs with other officials and bathing in Madeira wine. Ilse also had a reputation for being fascinated with tattoos, and when prisoners were discovered to have interesting tattoos or other birthmarks, those individuals frequently disappeared. Ilse reportedly developed a collection of tattoos on tanned human skin, which were turned into lampshades and other items, decorating her rooms, though some researchers question the accuracy of these allegations.

The Koch's reputation for ill-treatment soon became too much for even the Nazi high command, though it is possible that Karl-Otto's downfall was based more on his embezzlement of funds than it was for his inhuman treatment of prisoners. In any event, Karl-Otto did not survive the war, as his poor reputation led to him being removed from Buchenwald and given a different position, and in April of 1945, after being convicted by a Nazi court of charges connected to excessive brutality and murder and embezzlement, he received the death penalty by firing squad. Ilse was acquitted of similar charges, but after the war, she was tried and convicted of various atrocities. (It is obvious that the pair were particularly heinous people when the *Nazis* thought they were mistreating the people imprisoned in the camps!) Her life sentence was controversially reduced by General Lucius Clay, who believed that allegations of human skin lampshades and various acts of terrible treatment were false, though in later years, researchers verified some of the charges Clay dismissed. This led to a second trial, where Ilse was once again convicted and sentenced to life in jail in 1951, where she remained for sixteen and a half years before committing suicide by hanging.[4]

This is just a very brief overview of the atrocities of Buchenwald, and the omissions are due simply to the nature of this venue. There is a vast amount of scholarship on the horrors of the camp that is readily available to anyone who wishes to learn more about this monstrous period of history.

Moving back to prison life at Buchenwald, it is important to realize just how little there was to do in a P.O.W. camp, as well as how desperate prisoners were to be distracted from the constant barrages of brutality and death. Books were often scarce and were frequently confiscated. Board and card games could lose their appeal after a relatively short time, and conversational topics depleted quickly. P.O.W.'s with a background in certain topics might give lectures or teach classes. The bleakness of camp existence was pervasive and led to depression. Camps were jammed full of prisoners, often had terrible sanitation, and the food was rarely enjoyable or plentiful.[5]

Amateur theatricals and other performances were one of the few creative distractions available. Concentration camp amateur theatricals were performed by using whatever clothes and scraps of cloth were available for costumes, and usually using minimal sets. Interestingly, in some cases, guards were known to participate, sometimes in technical roles, sometimes in the cast, and more frequently as audience members.

Fris talks about how hard it was to find source material that appealed to the prisoners, and we may never know who brought a copy of *And Then There Were None* to the camp and smuggled it inside. Fris does not say what language the book was in, though it is notable that there was a German-language edition of *And Then There Were None* published during the war. Given the international situation, Christie would not have approved of her works being sold in enemy territory, and it is pretty certain that Christie never received any money from the wartime sales. Like many authors, in some nations, unauthorized versions of Christie's work would be sold, and unscrupulous publishers would keep all the profits for themselves. It is notable that there was a considerable audience for Christie's work in Germany at this time, despite the war.

Fris only gives some basic details about his reaction to the book, but it is interesting to see how the themes of justice outside of the law, the growing guilt of people who have gotten away with murder, and the general feeling of doom resonated with the inmates. Notably, Fris had trouble finding a proper work to adapt. There were countless other mysteries and thrillers that might have made it to the stage, yet as Fris said, nothing else felt "right." Yet *And Then There Were None*, certainly not a traditional mystery, had a special resonance. Could the inmates have seen the actions of Walter Sommer and

Karl-Otto and Ilse Koch reflected in the characters? Could the idea that somehow, somewhere, justice would be done against people who had taken human lives appeal to the prisoners? Might the depictions of a military man committing crimes on the battlefield, a judge sentencing a potentially innocent man to death, a policeman jailing someone who had done nothing wrong, a doctor killing a patient, and ordinary people standing idly by and allowing people to die have struck a chord with people who saw such actions happening in their own everyday lives? This is all speculation, but it's definitely possible that the prisoners took a level of comfort in a story that depicts long-delayed justice finally being carried out, forcing killers to confront their own consciences at long last and at great emotional pain. In any event, the prisoners responded very well to the play, according to Fris. There is no information as to how the prison guards responded to the play.

What happened after Agatha Christie received this letter? On a couple of Finnish mystery blogs, a handful of people repeat the same quote, stating that Christie's agent denied the request to stage the play, declaring that "business was business" and that an unauthorized adaptation could not be allowed to be performed. It is uncertain as to how this conclusion to the story came about, but as it seems to be only the one quote, shared amongst four blogs, this may be a bit of misinformation, though the origin of this tale is unknown. In contrast, the few English-language articles and essays that refer to this incident indicate that Christie happily granted permission, and the one-night-only production was a great success.[6]

Little is known about what happened to Fris after 1947, the names or fates of the other cast members, or if copies of the script still exist. There are a lot of unanswered questions, but hopefully, some enterprising Christie historian will be able to pursue this topic further in the future. Perhaps the Fris adaptation will be produced again at some point.

[1] Letter from G.W. Fris to Agatha Christie, April 23rd, 1947, The Agatha Christie Archive.

[2] "Buchenwald: The Statistics of Buchenwald," *Jewish Virtual Library*,

accessed July 6, 2025, https://www.jewishvirtuallibrary.org/the-statisti cs-of-buchenwald.

[3] David A. Hackett, translator, *The Buchenwald Report* (Basic Books, 1995), 1-424.

[4] Flint Whitlock, *The Beasts of Buchenwald: Karl & Ilse Koch, Human-skin Lampshades, and the War-crimes Trial of the Century* (Cable Publishing, 2011), Kindle.

[5] Flint Whitlock, *Buchenwald: Hell on a Hilltop* (Cable Publishing, 2013), Kindle.

[6] Morgan, 266.

Chapter Twenty-One

Kevin Elyot's Stage Adaptation

A good story can be told multiple times in different ways. Not only has *And Then Were None* seen multiple movie and television adaptations, but it has also received another authorized stage adaptation by the playwright Kevin Elyot. Elyot (1951-2014) was a playwright and actor who gained a reputation as one of the leading Christie adaptors for the screen, thanks to his work on the series *Agatha Christie's Poirot* and *Marple*. Elyot wrote the *Poirot* episode *Five Little Pigs* (2003), which is widely considered one of the series' finest episodes, and he also scripted the show's version of *Death on the Nile* (2004). His work was sufficiently revered that he was entrusted to write the series finale *Curtain: Poirot's Last Case* (2013). He also wrote six episodes of *Marple*: *The Body in the Library* (2004), *The Moving Finger* (2006), *Towards Zero* (2007), *A Pocket Full of Rye* (2008), *The Mirror Crack'd from Side to Side* (2010), and *Endless Night* (2013).[1]

Elyot's *And Then There Were None* premiered at the Gielgud Theatre in the West End on October 25, 2005, with previews starting on the 14th of the month. Its limited run was originally planned to end February 26, 2006, but it ended six weeks early on January 14, 2006. Not including an intermission, the show ran for two hours and ten minutes. The tagline in some advertisements was "Don't be trapped by the past..." illustrating the production's branding itself as a more modern take on the story. A frequently cited line was that the narrative had been given "a Tarantino twist."

The cast was as follows:

Dr. Edward Armstrong - Richard Clothier
Albert Blore - David Ross
Emily Brent - Gemma Jones
Vera Claythorne - Tara Fitzgerald
Captain Lombard - Anthony Howell
General Macarthur - Graham Crowden
Anthony Marston - Sam Crane
Rogers - John Ramm
Mrs. Rogers - Katy Brittain
Justice Wargrave - Richard Johnson[2]

Some of the actors had additional ties to Agatha Christie adaptations. Graham Crowden played Colonel Kingston Bruce in the Tommy & Tuppence series *Partners in Crime*, in the episode "The Affair of the Pink Pearl" (1983). Gemma Jones had a previous working relationship with Kevin Elyot while he was adapting Christie, playing Miss Williams in the *Poirot* episode *Five Little Pigs* (2003). Tara Fitzgerald also worked on an Elyot Christie adaptation previously, playing Adelaide Jefferson in the *Marple* episode *The Body in the Library* (2004), and later would play Lady Hermione in the three-part miniseries *The ABC Murders* (2018), scripted by Sarah Phelps. Some years later, Sam Crane would have a small part as Lieutenant Blanchflower in the *Poirot* episode *Murder on the Orient Express* (2010).[3]

Steven Pimlott directed the show, with Mark Thompson designing both the sets and the costumes, Hugh Vanstone designing the lighting, Jason Carr composing the original music, Gregory Clarke designing the sound, and Nick Hall handling the fight direction. The poster art featured "And Then There Were None" in large letters superimposed over a silhouette of a mountainous island, with the words illegibly reflected on the surface of the sea.

Though Elyot's adaptation followed Christie's novel closely, even including the original, darker ending, his play was quite different stylistically from Christie's work. There was no cameo role for an actor playing Fred Narracott, and instead of opening with the characters arriving on the island, the first scene was at the dinner table with all of the guests eating. Elyot's take on *And Then There Were None* put more emphasis on explicit material than Christie's script. The first death reflected how messy cyanide poisoning can be in real life, with Marston projectile vomiting as he died. Apparently, the mess was so severe that at one performance it required a three-minute pause to mop up the damage. Additionally, Vera did not simply dangle limply from the noose during her hanging, but instead she mimicked the death spasms of an actual hanged person. Shortly before the climax, Vera and Lombard had a physically intimate moment on the beach. At the end, Wargrave died from suicide rather than being killed by one of the other characters, and there were no survivors.

The set was designed in an elaborate Art Deco style, which would rotate to illustrate different rooms, with the rhyme displayed in large letters along a large pillar in the dining room. The term "soldiers" was used in the rhyme.[4]

The reviews were mixed. Some of the reviewers went out of their way to sneer at Agatha Christie and the whodunit genre in general, while others considered the play to be quite fun. Others were put off by the gore. In his history of Agatha Christie's dramatic work, *Curtain Up*, Julius Green was critical of the production, describing the Elyot adaptation as "unnecessary."[5]

As of this writing, Kevin Elyot's adaptation of *And Then There Were None* has not been produced since its initial run, is no longer authorized for performances, and the script has never been published. If one wants to read the playscript, one of the few copies available to the public can be found in Elyot's archived papers at the University of Bristol.[6] Theatre companies that wish to bring Christie's story to the stage must use Christie's own version.

[1] "Kevin Elyot," The Internet Movie Database, accessed July 4, 2025, https://www.imdb.com/name/nm0255946/?ref_=nv_sr_srsg_0_tt_0_nm _5_in_0_q_kevin%2520elyot.

[2] *"And Then There Were None (Kevin Elyot Adaptation),"* Agatha Christie Wiki, accessed July 4, 2025, https://agathachristie.fandom.com/wiki/And_Then_There_Were_None_(Kevin_Elyot_adaptation).

[3] The Internet Movie Database.

[4] Natalie Bennett, "Theatre Review: Agatha Christie's *And Then There Were None,*" *My London Your London,* December 28, 2005, https://mylondonyourlondon.com/?p=41.

[5] Julius Green, *Agatha Christie: A Life in Theatre: Curtain Up* (HarperCollins, 2015), Kindle.

[6] "Kevin Elyot Archive," *University of Bristol,* accessed July 4, 2025, https://www.bristol.ac.uk/theatre-collection/explore/theatre/kevin-elyot-archive/.

Chapter Twenty-Two

The Norwegian Opera

The parodic *Something's Afoot* notwithstanding, *And Then There Were None* was not adapted for musical theater until 2023, when Mathias Halvorsen created his second opera, crafting both the music and the libretto. The Norwegian-language show was commissioned by the Haugesund Kammeropera and the Haugesund Teater. Haugesund is located on the southwestern coast of Norway, a little south of Bergen. Morten Joachim Henriksen was the director. Gjermund Andresen designed the scenery. On his official website, Halvorsen describes the production, saying:

"The story is the quintessential horror crime story, with Christies original novel still being the best selling crime novel of all time. At the start of the opera a group of strangers are invited to an isolated island, when a storm hits. Very soon the guests start dying one by one, and they soon realise they are being hunted.

The libretto follows Christies play from 1939 quite closely, with only minor adjustments. Christies original language is the basis for the tone of the play, which is very humorous and light—at least in the first act. The music tries to mirror the tension of the situation, and often tries to enhance the contrast between mundane conversation (Would you like a drink? Whisky? Sherry?), and the highly dramatic and virtuosic medium opera can be. Hence, I often describe the style of the piece as self-ironic opera.

As the opera progresses and the bodies pile up, the tone turn darker, and the music turns more dramatic and less frivolous. The material is denser, and the use of pastiche elements from the first act is gone (almost). Some of the characters and their vocal parts go through drastic changes, while others seems not too affected by the terrifying situation they all of a sudden find themselves in."[1]

Described as a "comedic opera thriller in three acts," the show is about two hours long, with the first act being the longest, at fifty minutes. Act two is about half an hour, and the third act clocks in at twenty-five minutes.

Vera is sung by a mezzo singer, and the role can be doubled with Mrs. Rodgers (this is the spelling used in the show). Armstrong is played by a mezzo as well. Emily Brent is a soprano, as, surprisingly, is Blore, who is feminized here. Lombard and Marston are tenors, whereas Rodgers and Mackenzie are baritones. Mackenzie's role was designed for a non-trained singer, and was performed by one of the musicians in the original version of the show. The characters of Vera and Mrs. Rodgers can be doubled, as can Emily Brent and Blore, as well as Rodgers and Marston.

The parts were designed for performers with the following vocal capacities:

Vera Claythorne: Mezzo
Kaptein Lombard: Tenor
Dr. Armstrong: Mezzo
Judge Wargrave: Baritone
Emily Brent: Soprano
Davies/Blore: Soprano
Rodgers: Baritone
Anthony Marston: Tenor
Mrs. Rogers: Mezzo
General Mackenzie: Baritone[2]

Most of the costumes are relatively contemporary in style, and Emily Brent is dressed in black clericals and a white collar, while Mackenzie wore a military uniform. Jørgen Backer played an uncharacteristically young Dommer Wargrave, Lene Rudbæk was Vera, Andrè Søfteland played Alfred Rodgers, Janna Kari Kvinnesland was Ada Rodgers, Kjell Magnus Sandve played Kaptein Phillip Lombard, Mathilde Salmi Marjavara was Emily Brent, Nikolai Matthews played Mackenzie, and Ane Skumsvoll was Blore. The characters of Armstrong and Marston were doubled by members of the eight-person cast. During the production, musicians were visible onstage.[3]

As of this writing, an English translation is not available, and the possibility of further productions remains to be seen. No recording of the production has been released yet, either.

[1] Mathias Halvorsen, *"And Then There Were None,"* *Mathias Halvorsen,* accessed July 4, 2025, https://www.mathiashalvorsen.com/work#/and-then-there-were-none-1/. This is quoted directly from the autotranslation of the website, technical issues and all.

[2] Mathias Halvorsen.

[3] Karen Frøsland, "Nystøyl, Kriminelt kraftfull Agatha Christie-opera," NRK, accessed July 4, 2025, https://www.nrk.no/anmeldelser/anmeldelse_-_and-then-there-were-none_-pa-haugesund-teater-1.16387206.

IV

PART FOUR: Screen Adaptations

Chapter Twenty-Three

And Then There Were None (1945 feature film)

June Duprez: Vera Claythorne
Louis Hayward: Philip Lombard
Roland Young: Detective William Henry Blore
Walter Huston: Dr. Edward G. Armstrong
Barry Fitzgerald: Judge Francis J. Quincannon (Wargrave)
Judith Anderson: Emily Brent
Richard Haydn: Thomas Rogers
C. Aubrey Smith: General Sir John Mandrake (Macarthur)
Queenie Leonard: Ethel Rogers
Mischa Auer: Prince Nikita Starloff (Marston)
Harry Thurston: Fred Narracott
Directed by René Clair
Screenplay by Dudley Nichols[1]

The first filmed adaptation of *And Then There Were None* is still one of the best. Indeed, for many fans, it is *the* most enjoyable adaptation of her work. The movie is based more on Christie's stage adaptation than it is on her original novel, as it includes the "happy" ending with Lombard and Vera surviving and falling in love. The screenplay by Dudley Nichols (an Oscar-winner for 1936's *The Informer*, though he temporarily declined the award in an attempt to generate public support for the new Screen Writers Guild, and accepted a statuette later) became the template for the three later English-language feature films, which would borrow some of the little scenes and details he added to the narrative without crediting him.

Some of the changes included the names. The General became John Mandrake, and the Judge took on the new moniker Francis J. Quincannon. Both characters were slightly changed from their earlier incarnations. The General clearly suffers from senility from his earliest appearance, constantly mistaking Vera for his late wife, frequently misunderstanding words despite his hearing aid, and generally stumbling about in a fog. The Judge, based on Barry Fitzgerald's interpretation, is a warmer character than in the book. Instead of a dry, humorless figure of authority, this take on the Judge smiles frequently and has a twinkle in his eye much of the time. Though, as an older man, he is told by the Doctor to take care of his health with the potential onset of a cold, he is not the frail, limping figure depicted in other films. The Judge is sufficiently robust to join Lombard, Blore, and Doctor Armstrong on a search of the island.

The biggest change to a character is the transformation of Anthony Marston to Prince Nikita Starloff. Instead of a spoiled young Englishman, he is an excessively jovial middle-aged Russian aristocrat. Though his backstory is never clarified, it is implied that he was forced to flee his home country after the communist revolution, and now makes a living as a "professional guest," attending other people's parties and acting as an icebreaker who lightens the mood, though in practice, he puts others off with his copious drinking and his excessive high spirits.

Most of the other characters are essentially the same as in the play, although the Doctor is now depicted as a closet alcoholic, who hides his addiction (and his bottle and flask) early on before breaking down and drinking openly as the pressure increases. Additionally, Rogers, after he realizes he is the chief suspect, takes to drinking, and has a tipsy scene played for laughs before he goes out of the house to spend his last night on earth sleeping on a cot in the woodshed.

Bigger changes arise from the identities of the guests' victims.

Starloff/Marston's victims are now adults, rather than children. Vera's supposed victim is not a child under her care, but instead was the fiancé of her sister. It is later revealed that not only was Vera innocent of his death, but it was her sister who committed the crime. Finally, Emily Brent no longer drove a pregnant maid to suicide. Instead, she sent a troublemaking nephew to a reformatory, implied to be a horrible place, where he later took his own life.

Most of the deaths mirror the play, though the drunken Doctor is drowned in shallow water at the edge of the beach, rather than being pushed off a cliff and washed ashore later. Blore dies from a pyramid-shaped stone decoration being pushed down upon him, which ruins the rhyme, as it does not have anything to do with a bear. Finally, after the Judge confesses to Vera, he commits suicide by drinking fast-acting poison, and suggests that she commit suicide via a noose he has thoughtfully provided for her, rather than face an undignified trial and certain hanging, as she is the only person left alive on the island. The Judge's plans are shattered in his last moments, when Lombard appears seconds before the Judge dies, as he convinced Vera to fire away from him, and he simply pretended to die in order to trap U.N. Owen. Vera and Lombard are then set to live happily ever after when Narracott arrives to take them home.

There are several innovations that would be carried on into future adaptations. Lombard is actually not really Lombard, but a friend of the real Lombard who decided to investigate when his pal committed suicide after receiving the invitation. The first clue is early in the movie, when Lombard holds a suitcase with the initials "C.M." He tells Vera in the penultimate scene that his real name is Charles Morley. Other scenes that would be carried into future adaptations include the Prince/Marston singing the nursery rhyme at the piano, and a voting scene after the third murder, where the remaining seven vote for the most likely suspect. Vera receives no votes, and Rogers gets two, being declared the "winner," much to the butler's indignation. An earlier scene makes it clear who suspects whom in most cases, and though it is not spelled out, it is suggested that the judge voted for Rogers to isolate him before targeting him next. Another hallmark scene of the adaptation shows Blore trying and failing to fix a dying generator, inadvertently killing the power to the house. The judge and the doctor share a couple of scenes in the billiard room, and these exchanges will feature in future adaptations. In another new scene, halfway through the murders, the five remaining characters confess to the murders one by one, at the judge's instigation. The judge claimed he had nothing against the man he sentenced to death, but he forced a guilty verdict to ruin the reputation of a defense attorney. Though it is never spelled out in the film or subsequent adaptations, this may all be a lie in order to deflect suspicion. The doctor and Blore confess as well, and Lombard slyly refers to himself in the supposed third person, saying "Mr. Lombard" cannot deny his guilt. As the real Lombard's dead, he is able to make it sound like he's confessing while still telling the truth. Only Vera fails to make a confession, and it leads Armstrong to conclude she's U.N. Owen. One more recurring innovation consists of a house cat who wanders the grounds.

One minor question mark arises due to the figurines. The ten statuettes are each a little over a foot high, and are white china representations of Native Americans, arranged in a circle on a stand. After the first death, the figurine is broken on the table, with the base and feet remaining. Yet in later scenes, the shattered statuette has not been removed. Why would Rogers, who presumably tidied up the rest of the china shards, leave the feet with sharp points sticking up on the stand? Is it not more likely that, as a well-trained servant, he ought to have taken away every bit of the broken statuette? After the ensuing crimes, the figurines are mostly broken off at the ankles, and only the feet remain, though after Lombard's "death," all of the pieces of the shattered next-to-last figurine remain on the table. It is never made clear what happened to the other pieces of the broken statuettes.

Unlike later adaptations, which would stress darkness and moody suspense, the 1945 movie would incorporate some comedic scenes while still maintaining an apprehensive atmosphere and stressing psychological tension. A couple of scenes are played for pure comedy, such as one where Lombard, Blore, Armstrong, and the Judge spy on each other through keyholes and listen at doors, and follow one another around until they are all standing together in a line. As mentioned earlier, Rogers is given an extended drunk scene that is played for laughs, and the General's old-man doddering frailty is treated as a joke as well, though there is some pathos in his reflective moments shortly before his death, as he quietly wonders why his wife was unfaithful.

There are a few scenes that are subtle clues as to the identity of U.N. Owen. When Lombard, Blore, Armstrong, and the Judge are searching the island after the first two deaths, while Lombard peers over the edge of a precipice over the sea, he declares that "Mr. Owen's hand is plain to see." Lombard is only visible from the shoulders up, and the only other character in the shot is the Judge, who is holding on to his hat with his hand clearly showing. A moment later, there is a close-up of the Judge, with both hands raised as he clutches his hat, protecting it from the coastal winds.

In a similar vein, shortly before the General's body is discovered, Lombard stares out of the dining room window into the rain and states, "all we have to do is keep quiet and we'll hear Mr. Owen sneeze." Several minutes later, after the Judge, Armstrong, Blore, and Lombard return from the woodshed after giving the key to the dining room to Rogers, the Judge gives a massive sneeze, and the D octor warns him about how many people are killed annually by the common cold. The sneeze takes place long enough after Lombard's lines that most viewers will forget all about it, and even those that do might not make the connection.

A third clue comes from the discovery of the Judge's body. Until his death, all of the murders are handled delicately. When Prince Nikita falls after being poisoned, his corpse is hidden by a large piece of furniture. Mrs. Rogers and the General's bodies are never seen. We see a bit of Rogers' feet and one of Miss Brent's hands after they are killed, but that is it. There is no gore, and hardly any bodies on-screen to speak of at all. It is therefore out of place when a big circular bullet hole appears in the middle of the Judge's forehead. No other corpse's face is ever shown on-screen (the Doctor is shown briefly face down in the wet sand, and barely any of Blore appears after he is crushed by the big stone ornament. By this depiction of a taboo subject—a murdered corpse's face, it is an indication that the Judge is not actually dead after all. After the Judge drinks poison at the end and dies for real, the camera keeps off him just as it did with the others.[2]

The 1945 version is a classic, but great stories often produce multiple adaptations, and over the decades, several other creative teams would adapt *And Then There Were None* to varying degrees of success.

[1] *"And Then There Were None (1945),"* *The Internet Movie Database*, accessed July 4, 2025, https://www.imdb.com/title/tt0037515/?ref_=ttfc_ov_bk.

[2] *And Then There Were None*, directed by René Clair (Twentieth Century Fox, 1945), 1 hr., 37 min., https://www.amazon.com/Then-There-Were-N one/dp/B08678Z4M1/ref=sr_1_2?crid=3SVU3BNA4YLH&dib=eyJ2Ijoi MSJ9.uzTkKnboKoaiz3i-d5w5zuqqIf3nHWcwAlwI984nP0QZlMxOmBw VY57aOcikjL3GNZENRfYkcElODEBa8ru2upyiOizGj7XJtiPogyDLByPcV iiqRCgGjhp-guUTemYqxOFhguoPO5Us2DFCiExBSm8saLJbmRIXCEpzq Cwef-26ElDyrthmuN3k-UdNZvUUwZSQ1Pwnaiq-pk0jXRPEqgOjbC0F N1iIPyQxwd3hjRg.RoLsZxcgqj1dGF851obKpJDfFBQ0lSiWk0v5hSS_Kj8 &dib_tag=se&keywords=and+then+there+were+none+1945&qid=175163 7574&s=movies-tv&sprefix=and+then+there+were+none+19%2Cmovies-tv%2C820&sr=1-2.

Chapter Twenty-Four

Ten Little Indians (1959 NBC Television Movie)

Nina Foch: Vera Claythorne

Kenneth Haigh: Philip Lombard

James Kenny (aka James Berwick) Det. William Henry Blore

Romney Brent: Dr. Edward Armstrong

Barry Jones: Mr. Justice Sir Lawrence Wargrave

Valerie French: Emily Brent

George Turner: Thomas Rogers

Peter Bathurst: General John Gordon Mackenzie (Macarthur)

Caroline Brenner: Ethel Rogers

Chandler Cowles: Frederick James Marston

Jeremiah Morris: Boatman

Directed by Paul Bogart, Philip F. Falcome, and Leo Farrenkopf

Screenplay by Philip H. Reisman Jr.[1]

In 1959, a one-hour television adaptation, titled *Ten Little Indians*, aired on NBC in the United States. It is one of the few filmed versions of *And Then There Were None* to air on television during this period to survive and be available for viewing. In 1983, it was released on VHS by Video Yesteryear, was later sold as a DVD, and became available for streaming on Amazon in the 21st century.

The quality is rather grainy, and the black-and-white footage is sometimes faded and washed out in places, making it difficult to see certain details, and there is some crackling in the sound.

The production was sponsored by the pharmacy chain Rexall Drugs, and the commercials are included in the recording. One of the commercials features a female announcer explaining what wonderful deals the drugstores have, while a pair of people in an elephant costume perform in the background. Some of the items on sale are highlighted, and Rexall offers a free bank shaped like an elephant with the purchase of certain products. As items and their corresponding deals are profiled, coins representing the savings are dropped into one of the elephant banks.

In the opening, Fred Narracott takes six of the guests on the boat to the island. Unlike the original book and most of the adaptations, Vera and Lombard are already on the island, along with Mr. and Mrs. Rogers, when the other six guests arrive. Vera and Lombard were strangers before arriving, but have already become friendly, much to the annoyance of Marston, who has a libidinous interest in Vera. During their first moment alone together, he propositions her, asking her if he can come to her room. She rebuffs him. Later, Marston suggests to Lombard that out of fairness, Lombard should give Marston a shot with Vera, smugly declaring that she will be unable to resist his luxury car. Lombard chooses not to engage with him, and Marston's attempts to pressure him are interrupted by the other guests.

The following original rhyme is spoken by an unseen narrator during the opening:

"Once upon an island, and once upon a time, off the coast of Devon, according to the rhyme: Ten little Indians, though the invitation said for fun, were invited to be murdered, one by one by one." This bit of doggerel is unique to this television, but there are several other heavily edited rhymes in this adaptation. In some cases, just one or two words of the poem are altered, in others, the entire content has been revised.

Like many of the adaptations, the rhyme is not read aloud all at once, and only the first two couplets are read before the murders occur, so the rhymes are recited right after some murders, and sometimes not at all. Marston and Mrs. Rogers meet their deaths as they do in the book, and to an essentially similar rhyme, but Mrs. Rogers' poison must have worked a lot faster than it did in the book, as she is discovered dead moments after Marston's body hits the floor. Two figurines are found shattered at the same time. The "Indians" in this adaptation appear to be Asian rather than American, and feature turbans with large plumes.

Shortly after the third murder, Vera recites the rhyme, but the sound is poor, and it is hard to make out some words. One potential interpretation of what she's saying is:

Eight little Indians stuffed all together (or possibly, "stuck down in Devon")

One swirled (this second word is unclear) and caught fire, and then there were seven.

Almost uniquely amongst the adaptations, the order of the victims has been changed. Rogers is the third victim rather than the General. Right before the search of the house, Wargrave tells Rogers to stoke the fire, and not long afterwards, Vera discovers Rogers dead in the study, struck over the head with the fireplace poker. His lifeless body was pitched forward into the flames, fitting the changed rhyme.

The next couplet is similarly original due to the fact that it actually combines two murders.

Seven little Indians very much alive,

Two missed their dinner and then there were only five.

General Mackenzie is found dead at a desk, having written a confession to sending a soldier who was having an affair with his wife to a location that their own side was bombarding. Blore thinks it is a suicide, but then Wargrave observes that the killer did not allow the General to take his own way out, and there is a knife in the General's back. When Vera searches for candles so as to have more light to study the crime scene, Miss Brent's body topples out of the wardrobe, strangled with what appears to be a scarf, though the quality of the recording makes the precise murder weapon uncertain. A few more details were added to Miss Brent's crime, as the young woman she drove to suicide was actually having an affair with Miss Brent's brother, and gave birth to his child. This adaptation is the only one to include the dead woman's baby in the record's accusation, as the infant died of unspecified causes soon after its mother's suicide, thereby charging Miss Brent with two deaths instead of one.

The General gets a substantial scene with Lombard earlier in the telemovie, where it's explained that he served in Mesopotamia (which he affectionately refers to as "the mess pot") during the First World War, and was sidelined at a desk during World War Two. It is implied that this was because of the death he deliberately caused. The General is portrayed as a bluff, yet generally amiable elderly man whose mind is just starting to fray around the edges. He seems reasonably sharp at first, though his memory fades with each scene. When the others discover his body, he has written a suicide note confessing to his responsibility for his wife's lover's death, but then the killer stuck a knife into his back before he could take his own life.

In contrast, Miss Brent is never more venomous than in this adaptation. Her religiosity has been stripped away, but her prudishness and self-righteousness are dialed up to eleven. When Vera shows Miss Brent to her room, Miss Brent treats Vera as a servant, compelling her to take her luggage, and barely deigning to favor her with a glance, until she actually shouts at Vera for wearing too tight a dress, which she finds offensive. The scene is almost comical in the over-the-top denunciation. From the vitriol, one would think that Vera was wearing a form-fitting dress with plunging cleavage and a hemline ending way above the knee, but it is actually a pretty modest black dress with a white collar. If Miss Brent wanted Vera to wear something less clingy Vera would have to slip into a circus tent. Vera thinks about changing, but then decides not to, and makes a point of rubbing this fact in Miss Brent's face.

The next couplet now contains the words "One became a Brahmin," and when Wargrave "dies," the supposed bullet hole in his head represents a bindi mark worn on the forehead, a decoration that is not exclusive to the Brahmin. The rest of the film unfolds very much like in the play, with the next two deaths matching the source material. Armstrong meets his fate in the sea, Blore is killed by a stone sculpture perched on the ledge on the outside of the front door, though it looks a bit more like a standard gargoyle than a bear. After he dies, Vera and Lombard both fall asleep in the lounge—

though on different pieces of furniture. When they awaken, it is a bright and sunny morning. The ending matches the original play, with Lombard firing the final shot that kills Wargrave, who devolves into a frenzied madman in his final scene. Instead of three stressful days, the events of this adaptation take less than eighteen hours to unfold, and seven of the deaths occur before morning. As for Vera and Lombard, all presumably ends happily for them.[2]

[1] *"Ten Little Indians (1959),"* *The Internet Movie Database*, accessed July 4, 2025, https://www.imdb.com/title/tt0278766/?ref_=fn_all_ttl_1.

[2] *Ten Little Indians*, directed by Paul Bogart, Philip F. Falcone, Leo Farrenkopf, and Dan Zampino, 1959, 1 hr., (Video Yesteryear, 2008), DVD.

Chapter Twenty-Five

Ten Little Indians (1965 Feature Film)

Shirley Eaton: Ann Clyde

Hugh O'Brian: Hugh Lombard

Stanley Holloway: William Blore

Dennis Price: Dr. Armstrong

Wilfrid Hyde-White: Judge Cannon (Wargrave)

Daliah Levi: Ilona Bergen (Brent)

Mario Adorf: Herr Grohmann (Rogers)

Leo Genn: General Mandrake (Macarthur)

Marianne Hoppe: Frau Grohmann (Mrs. Rogers)

Fabian: Mike Raven (Marston)

Bill Mitchell: Narrator of "Whodunit Break"

Christopher Lee: Voice of Mr. U.N. Owen

Directed by George Pollock

Screenplay by Peter Yeldham and Harry Alan Towers (writing under the name Peter Welbeck)[1]

Two decades after the first English-language adaptation of *And Then There Were None*, prolific producer Harry Alan Towers decided the time was ripe for a reimagined remake of the film. Co-writing the screenplay with Peter Yeldham (Towers used his pseudonym Peter Welbeck for the scripting credit), the 1965 script drew heavily from both the 1945 movie, as well as the play and original novel. George Pollock, who had directed all four Miss Marple movies starring Margaret Rutherford earlier in the decade, helmed the production.

The first and most obvious change is the location, as the setting is no longer an island off the coast of Devon, but instead is a luxurious chalet in the mountains of central Europe. The precise location is never mentioned explicitly, but some comments made by the servants, referencing their original location and the time it took to get to the chalet, suggest that the setting is very likely in the Alps.

There are a lot of name changes, as Vera Claythorne is now Ann Clyde. Wargrave is now Judge Cannon (abridging the "Quincannon" of the 1945 film). General Macarthur retains the 1945 film's surname of "Mandrake." Mr. and Mrs. Rogers are now central Europeans, Herr and Frau Grohmann. Emily Brent becomes Ilona Bergen, and Anthony Marston now bears the name of Mike Raven. Lombard's first name is now "Hugh," matching the actor who plays him.

Notably, a lot of the characterizations have been drastically altered as well. Lombard is much the same, aside from being given a new job as an engineer. Ann/Vera is still intelligent, though she is frequently shaken by anxiety and fear, but this characterization is by far the most sultry and sexualized version of the character ever. If the Miss Brent from the 1959 one-hour American television production thought that Vera's dress was offensively tight, she'd be apoplectic at various scenes where Ann is seen in her underwear, asking Lombard to zip up the back of her dress, and walking around her room in only a towel. Her clothing indicates that the setting has been moved to the 1960s as Ann's clothes reflect the styles of the time. Her initial outfit consists of a leather trench coat, a long black leather skirt, and a black turtleneck, and later ensemble choices include dresses in 1960's styles, and a couple of winter outdoor outfits.

Mike Raven is a moderately successful musician who thinks he is more famous than he really is. His musical take on the nursery rhyme is not well-received by the other guests, and his attempts to hit on Ilona are rebuffed—she dismisses him as beneath her, and suggests he try his luck with Ann.

Shortly before his death, he is visibly intoxicated, and he has undone his bow tie; exhibiting behavior that is much more gauche than in other versions.

Frau Grohmann is far gruffer and tougher than in previous incarnations, and is reminiscent of a more restrained predecessor of Cloris Leachman's Frau Blucher from *Young Frankenstein.* Tight-lipped, openly resentful of having to look after eight guests and a massive house, Frau Grohmann is a good deal angrier than the standard take on Mrs. Rogers, for after Ilona treats her disrespectfully, she calls Ilona a "bitch" the moment the guest leaves the room. She does get visibly agitated after the accusations are played. Her husband is much gruffer and prone to anger than the more proper takes on Mr. Rogers. Herr Grohmann's short temper leads to a fistfight with Lombard, where the butler does not quite fight fair, and takes a nasty beating after a couple of minutes of brawling.

The Judge, the Doctor, and Blore are very close to their earlier incarnations, but the General is not the least bit senile, and though he is an older man, he is sharp, dignified, and courtly. It is Ilona whose character is the most radically changed. No longer a condemning religious zealot, the character has been de-aged a couple of decades and transformed into a glamorous actress with an unrequited attraction to Lombard. After Lombard defeats the butler in a fight, Ilona's visibly aroused.

Most of the people the guests are accused of murdering are the same as the ones in the 1945 version, though the woman Lombard is accused of driving to suicide is explicitly stated to be bearing his child out of wedlock. The General is not accused of sending his wife's lover to die, but instead, through bad judgment and cowardice, led five of his men to their deaths, and was decorated and promoted because no one knew the truth. It seems that Lombard's original crime has been revised a bit and transferred to the General. Ilona Bergen is accused of killing her husband with cruelty. Stuck in Central Europe, she married her British soldier husband in order to advance her acting career. Once her husband's connections led to an offer in Hollywood, she informed her spouse that she never loved him and that the wedding was solely one of convenience for her. (This might be a riff on a comparable plot point in *Witness for the Prosecution.*) Broken-hearted, her husband picked up a shotgun and took his own life. A minor subplot has the General previously acquainted with Ilona, as he was her husband's commanding officer. The couple Mike Raven runs over are adults, not children, as in the 1945 movie.

The characters are mostly dispatched as they were in the 1945 version, with a few exceptions. A few of the couplets of the rhyme have been changed, sometimes by a dropped or single changed word, though three early couplets are heavily altered:

Nine little Indians staying up quite late,

One went away and then there were eight.

Eight little Indians traveling to Heaven,

One met a pussycat and then there were seven.

Seven little Indians chopping sticks,

The chopper finished one of them and then there were six.

The first and most dramatic alteration to the murders is to the housekeeper's death. Frau Grohmann is far more outspoken than the traditional interpretation of Mrs. Rogers, and she repeatedly berates her husband, claiming that they should never have taken this new job, and ought to have stayed in Vienna. A couple of comments make it obliquely but unambiguously clear that they are indeed guilty of the crime of which they are accused, but they never confess in front of the other guests. Rather incongruously, during the accusation scene (instead of a record, the accusation is modernized into a reel of audio tape, and it is voiced by an uncredited Christopher Lee), the Grohmanns simply stand around taking care of their household duties for most of the recording's run time. It is not until they are named at the very end that they are shocked by the charge against them. It is rather out of place that Frau Grohmann, in particular, should look so blindsided, as they should have realized that if everybody else in the room was being accused of getting away with murder, that it was only a matter of time before their turn arrived. Why would she assume that the staff would be ignored?

The second couplet is changed to "one fell down." Frau Grohmann, realizing that it is not safe at the chalet, decides to get out while the going's good, and takes the funicular by herself. Unfortunately, someone has frayed the cable that allows the carriage to glide down to the base of the mountain, and midway through the ride, the cord snaps, sending the funicular and the housekeeper plunging to the ground.

The viewer knows that Frau Grohmann almost certainly dies here, as the camera shows the frightened woman in the shaking carriage moments before it hurtles to the earth. However, the witnesses to her demise, Ann, Lombard, and Herr Grohmann, really don't know for sure that her life ended at that moment. As none of the three (or anybody else that we know of) actually saw her getting into the funicular, and they can't get a good look at her from this distance, it's possible that she is not in there at all and that the shadow they see is just a dummy. Theoretically, Frau Grohmann could have set the booby-trapped funicular going without her in it, and then hid somewhere. As they never recover her body, it is certainly possible, as far as the guests know, that Frau Grohmann is the killer. Yet no one posits this theory, which, even though the viewer knows that it is false, could, as far as the guests know, be true.

The General, sharp and competent, organizes the search of the house. Once they examine the chalet from top to bottom, they all end up in the labyrinthine cellar, and divide up into pairs. The General pressures Ilona to confide in him, but she runs off without admitting anything, foolishly leaving both the General and herself alone. The other pairs get separated as well, leaving no one with an alibi when the pet cat that lives at the chalet approaches the General. His last action on earth is to pick it up and pet it, as the killer then stabs him, presumably in the front. The knife in question is taken from a collection of weapons framed upon the wall.

Like his wife, Herr Grohmann dies by falling off the mountain. At five A.M. the following morning, he gathers up some mountain climbing equipment and attempts a dangerous descent down a sheer cliff. Unfortunately for him, his safety precautions are rendered moot when the killer takes a hatchet and chops his rope in two, sending him hurtling to the ground. The location is a bit difficult to reach, so it is surprising that the killer was able to make it to an awkward spot on the rock in order to chop the rope. More frustrating is the fact that none of the guests ever see the body. They simply notice his absence, hear Lombard announce that a fourth figurine is missing, and most are swiftly convinced that the butler is dead, despite Blore suspecting a trick. The cleverer guests ought to be considering the possibility that he is still alive and is still targeting them for death. Really, since neither of the Grohmann's bodies are discovered, the guests should never stop considering that one or both of the servants could be simply hiding. However, after a few moments of suspicion, none of the guests worries about the absent servants.

Ilona's manner of death remains the same as Miss Brent's, though the poison in the syringe is not specified, and no live bee is present. She dies in her bedroom, and it is revealed that a little circle of embroidered bumblebees is stitched upon the quilt of the bed of her room, where she dies. Unlike in the book, she is not doped into unresponsiveness beforehand, and though she sees the deadly hypodermic pointed in her direction, she does not scream loudly to summon the others. Blore's death fits the rhyme far better than in the 1945 version, as a large statue of a bear, featured in the background of several scenes, is tossed off the roof right onto his head. As there is no large body of water around, Doctor Armstrong does not drown. He is simply lured off to a secluded clearing and is later found face down in the snow. No specific manner of death is ever clarified.

Right before the judge's supposed death, Ann leaves to get her coat from her room, but the reason for her screaming and sending the men running upstairs is not seaweed hanging from a hook, but a statuette of a Native American hanging from a thread, brushing against her face. It is rather larger than the ten statuettes that are broken off with each murder.

The figurines are small, Native Americans in various poses, such as pointing drawn bows and arrows, and each figurine is affixed to a circular base. After each murder, one is broken off, leaving just the feet behind on the base. What happens to the top ninety percent of the broken figurines is not shown. Initially, the platter with the ten figures is used to serve fruit at the end of dinner. The final shot of the film is of the platter, with two intact figures left, with the cat lying next to them.

One major change is the addition of a physical relationship between Ann and Hugh. Shortly after the judge is supposedly shot, the doctor accuses Ann, as in the 1945 film, she is the only one who has not confessed to murder, so paradoxically, she is the chief suspect. The doctor insists on locking Ann in her room, but Lombard keeps the key and lets himself inside. He earns her trust by tossing her the gun, and she is so relieved by this she leaps into her arms. When Lombard convinced Vera to let him into her room in the 1945 version by offering her the gun, their following interaction was restrained and chaste. Twenty years later, the pair passionately kiss and have sex in Ann's bed.

Another gimmick added to the climax was the "Whodunit Break," which is deleted from the current DVD release of the film, though it is included as a special feature. When Ann and Hugh discover the doctor's body and believe that they are the only two remaining, Ann points the revolver at Hugh, but cannot bring herself to shoot as Hugh tries to convince her that they are missing something.

"Ladies and gentlemen, let us pause to consider the plight of these two people, who were learning how to trust each other. Now, for the first time in motion pictures, we offer you a "Whodunit Break," a brief intermission in which to reflect. Who is the murderer of eight people? Is it Ann Clyde? Hugh Lombard? Or have eight people really been killed? Do you think you know the answer? Don't be too certain. Why not think about it for just one minute? Turn to the person in the seat next to you, and for the next sixty seconds, discuss who the murderer might be while we refresh your memory with a few clues."

The words "Whodunit Break" flash across the screen briefly after the onscreen action freezes, and a clock appears in the center of the screen, with a single hand counting down the seconds. A series of clips, beginning with Raven playing the rhyme on the piano, are shown. After the guests react to the tape recording, Raven chokes and dies. Interestingly, the next scenes are shown out of order. The General's stabbing comes next, followed by the crashing of the funicular, though Frau Grohmann is not shown in the car in this clip, just the wire fraying and Ann, Hugh, and Grohmann looking on in horror. Next comes the hatchet-wielding hand chopping Grohmann's mountain-climbing rope and his subsequent fall, followed by

Ilona gasping in fear at the approaching hypodermic needle. The fired gun and the discovery of the judge in his bedroom are next, and then the bear statue is shown hurtling towards Blore. Next, Hugh and Ann discover the doctor's body, and the last ten seconds of the minute are devoted to their bedroom scene.

The clock chimes, and the narrator says, *"Your time is up, ladies and gentlemen. We've given you the opportunity to solve the mystery. But we doubt that you've guessed right. Don't be surprised at the next thing you see."* The action resumes, showing Ann firing the gun and Hugh falling.

The selected clips do provide some clues. As the clips show an unknown hand stabbing the General, cutting Grohmann's ropes, injecting Ilona, and pushing the bear statue at Blore, it's shown that those four cannot be the killer, as their deaths were caused by someone else's hand. But the firing of the gun is not done with the judge visible in the scene, so the video evidence does not exonerate him.

A 2012 Region 1 DVD release cuts the "Whodunit Break" from the movie, and the shot of Ann and Hugh in the snow proceeds uninterrupted to Ann pulling the trigger. The "Whodunit Break" is included as a DVD special feature.

The denouement plays out just like in the 1945 version, with the Judge playing billiards, confessing, drinking poison, and then dying just as he sees Lombard alive and realizes that his plans are ruined, and his last words are from the 1945 version, grumbling about never trusting women. The final shot is of the cat lying next to the nearly destroyed centerpiece, though two figurines remain intact.

This is the only filmed adaptation with the "happy" ending that does not end with the two survivors getting rescued. It is implied that the two of them will be saved once the villagers attempt to deliver supplies and see the damaged funicular, but it is unclear just how Lombard and Ann will get away, as it will be difficult to repair the funicular. Perhaps a helicopter will be chartered to pick them up and carry them home.

[1] *"Ten Little Indians (1965),"* *The Internet Movie Database,* accessed July 5,

2025, https://www.imdb.com/title/tt0061075/?ref_=nv_sr_srsg_0_tt_8_nm_0_in_0_q_ten%2520little%2520indians.

Chapter Twenty-Six

Gumnaam (1965 Indian Musical Adaptation)

Nanda Karnataki (as Nanda): Asha
Manoj Kumar (as Manoj): Anand
Pran Sikhand (as Pran): Barrister Rakesh
Helen: Miss Kitty
Mehmood: The Butler
Dhumal: Mister Dharamdas
Madan Puri: Dr. Acharya
Tarun Bose: Madhusudan Sharma
Manmohan: Mr. Kishan
Naina: Unnamed Woman
Directed by Raja Nawathe
Screenplay by Dhruva Chatterjee
Story and Dialogue by Charandas Shokh[1]

Agatha Christie is one of the very few writers who has global popular appeal. Christie has fans worldwide, and it's not surprising that moviemakers from non-English-speaking countries might want to adapt her books for the screen while adjusting the plots to reflect their own cultural backgrounds. This was the case with *Gumnaam* (Anonymous), a Bollywood Hindi-language film that made heavy adjustments to Christie's narrative while keeping much of the familiar structure intact. Christie was not credited for this adaptation.

The film opens with a man named Sohanlal being run down by a car in the street. His business associate, Khanna, is behind the crime, and Khanna makes several phone calls to individuals who are assisting him in various ways in his plot for profit. Though only the hands and arms of most of the people on the other end of the line are only shown on-screen, holding the phones, it is soon implied that these people are the guests to the island. The last person to be called is the only one whose face is shown—Asha, Sohanlal's niece. She is genuinely distraught by the news of her uncle's death, and she's even more upset when she hears gunfire on the other end of the line. A person wearing a long coat, whose face is (unsurprisingly) not shown, has killed Khanna.

After the opening credits, the action moves to a nightclub where an elaborate and boisterous dance scene to the song "Jaan Pehechan Ho" is performed by masked dancers and a similarly masked singer. The song and the movie clip feature in the opening credits of the 2001 American movie *Ghost World*, where the main character dances boisterously to the movie. This musical number does not seem to be directly connected to the plot, but it is an energetic start to the film. There are some numbering parallels, as there are ten male and ten female chorus dancers in addition to the female star dancer, and most of the entertainers wear masks for most of the performance. It should be noted that on the only official DVD release available in the U.S., there are English subtitles for the dialogue but not the song lyrics, so it is possible that there may be some clues in various song lyrics that escape viewers that do not know Hindi.

At the nightclub, seven patrons: Asha, Dr. Acharya, Dharamdas, Kitty, Kishan, Barrister Rakesh, and Madhusudan Sharma; win a luxury vacation. However, as they are all flown out on the trip, the plane allegedly develops engine trouble, and they are forced to land in a field on a mysterious island. The seven guests and a member of the plane's crew, Anand, leave the plane and step aside to wait, but soon after the group walks a short distance away, the plane takes off, leaving their luggage in the field. The eight shocked people gather their belongings and start walking in search of shelter, and in the woods, they hear a woman's voice singing, but they cannot actually see the singer. They follow the voice through the woods, up rocky terrain, and by the time it gets dark, they arrive at a huge mansion.

There, they are greeted by the butler (known only by his job title), who has been expecting them. Their first night at the mansion gets off to a rocky start, as Dharamdas discovers a little book at the dinner table, accusing all of them of criminal activity connected to the events at the start of the film, and threatening their lives.

Over the course of the film, characters are targeted one by one. There is no nursery rhyme that gives the murders a theme, as the characters are stabbed, struck, and strangled. The crimes are punctuated by various musical numbers, many of which seem to take place in the imaginations of the characters, aside from a ghostly tune sung by a woman in the distance. The surroundings, both real and imagined, feature a lot of religious imagery from various backgrounds, including a real-life ruined Christian church filled with statues, and an imaginary pool setting filled with Muslim symbols. As the movie progresses, and the number of characters dwindles, the remaining characters grow increasingly nervous, some drinking to excess to escape the stress, and at one point, Asha hallucinates the ghosts of the dead coming towards her.

Eventually, when it seems like only Anand, Asha, and the butler are left, the supposedly dead Mr. Sharma is revealed to be alive, having faked his own death with the help of the doctor. Not only is Sharma not dead, but he is also much younger than he appears, having aged himself with a wig and makeup. He is really Madanial, a criminal who has fled custody, and who worked for a criminal gang run by the individuals in the movie's opening scenes. As his former associates betrayed him and destroyed his family, Madanial decided to kill them and those who helped them, rigging the contest to bring them all to the island. While the others were in some way complicit with the crimes, Asha was unaware of the illegality of her relative's actions, and Anand reveals that he is actually a police officer investigating the case. The butler is a completely innocent servant hired to take care of the guests, and he only violated his unknown employer's instructions in one way: he was told to come alone to the island, but as he had a mentally disabled sister who needed constant care, he took her along. It is the butler's sister who's been providing the disembodied singing voice the whole time.

Even though Asha and Anand did not do anything to harm him, Madanial ties them up and plays a game of Russian roulette with them in an underground chamber. Just as he's running out of empty chambers, the butler slips inside and frees Anand. As Anand and Madanial fight, the butler unties Asha. Madanial breaks away from Anand and tries to flee, but the authorities arrive by plane and capture him. Anand, Asha, the butler, and his sister hurry aboard the plane, leaving their luggage behind at the mansion.

As the film ends, the remaining five characters fly away to safety, a much larger group of survivors than in most versions of *And Then There Were None*.

None of the characters are closely based on the original *And Then There Were None* victims. While there are seven men and three women, the connections are tenuous. Asha is comparable to a movie version of Vera, and Anand is a more straitlaced version of Lombard. The butler is a much purer-hearted and jollier man than Rogers, and his sister is given no character development other than her mental state and propensity for singing. Neither sibling has been accused of any wrongdoing. The doctor likes to drink, though Sharma is not very much like Wargrave other than being the "elder statesman" of the group. A subtle clue that he is younger than he seems occurs when he breaks up a fight, and Kitty admiringly complements him on being stronger than his age would suggest. The coquettish good-time girl Kitty has no points of similarity with the original Emily Brent, but she is comparable to the youthful actress reimagining who was introduced in the 1965 version, though, as the movies were released in the same year, it is unclear if one influenced the other or if the de-aging change is simply a coincidence. Barrister Rakesh, Dharamdas, and Kishan are not direct parallels to Marston, Macarthur, and Blore.

The movie also addresses racial issues, as in one brief scene, where the lighter-skinned Kitty speaks derisively of the butler's dark skin, and the butler denounces prejudice based on melanin content. The butler also has some choice words about the class system as well, criticizing how the guests all demand different foods and then rarely appreciate them or even finish their meals, showing little respect for the one man tasked with catering to all of their needs.[2]

The film earned a few nominations at the 13th Filmfare Awards, which celebrate Hindi movies. S.S. Samel won for Best Art Director-Color, and Mehmood and Helen were nominated for their supporting roles. The catchy songs and dance numbers have earned numerous fans amongst Western audiences as well. A Tamil-language adaptation of *Gumnaam, Naalai Unathu Naal,* was released in 1984.[3]

[1] "Gumnaam (1965)," directed by Raja Nawathe, *The Internet Movie Database,* accessed July 5, 2025, https://www.imdb.com/title/tt024739 4/?ref_=nv_sr_srsg_7_tt_7_nm_1_in_0_q_gumnam.

[2] *Gumnaam,* directed by Raja Nawathe, Prithvi Pictures, 1965, 2 hrs. 31 min., (EROS), DVD.

[3] "Gumnaam (1965)."

Chapter Twenty-Seven

Ten Little Indians (1974 Feature Film)

Elke Sommer: Vera Clyde (Claythorne)
Oliver Reed: Hugh Lombard
Gert Fröbe: Blore
Herbert Lom: Dr. Armstrong
Richard Attenborough: Judge Cannon (Wargrave)
Stéphane Audran: Ilona (Brent)
Alberto de Mendoza: Martino (Rogers)
Adolfo Celi: The General
Maria Rohm: Elsa Martino (Mrs. Rogers)
Charles Aznavour: Raven (Marston)
Orson Welles: The Voice of U.N. Owen
Teresa Gimpera: Maria (Cut from English-language version)
Rik Battaglia (as Rick Battaglia): Vendedor (Cut from English-language version)
Directed by Peter Collinson
Screenplay by Harry Alan Towers (writing under the name Peter Welbeck), Erich Kröhnke and Enrique Llovet)[1]

Harry Alan Towers knew that he had a valuable property in the film rights to *And Then There Were None*, and over the course of more than two decades, he did everything he could to make the most out of this asset. Having produced a remake of the venerable story nine years earlier, Towers set out to try again. This time, instead of the traditional island off England's southern coast, or an isolated chalet in the snowy mountains, the action was transposed to an out-of-the-way hotel in the middle of the Iranian desert, and the story appears to be set around the time of filming.

The beautifully decorated hotel is surrounded by two hundred miles of desert on every side. The two servants are already there, and the housekeeper stands outside to greet the other eight guests, who arrive via helicopter. As lovely as the hotel is, there must not be reliable central heating, as most of the characters wear their coats inside on multiple occasions. The 1965 screenplay serves as a general template for this remake. Though several of the details of the deaths, a few names and ethnicities, and numerous lines of dialogue have been altered, the general narrative remains the same as it does in the earlier movie, without the one-minute pause at the end to allow the viewer to hypothesize upon the killer's identity.

In this adaptation, the figurines are of Asian Indian men, wearing turbans, white shirts, and brown pants, all circled around a centerpiece shaped like a palm tree. After every murder, one figurine is broken, sometimes at the waist, sometimes a bit higher or lower. Some of the figurines are broken off at the ankles, while others keep their legs and even parts of their chests. The damage changes from shot to shot, as the statuette broken after Elsa Martino's (Mrs. Rogers) murder is broken diagonally across the chest, but when the figures are shown after the General's death, there are two pairs of feet, and one statuette broken at the waist, along with seven intact figures.

The screenplay largely uses the 1965 movie's dialogue, with only a handful of changes and updates here and there accounting for different murder methods, the nationalities of the actors, and the 1970s. Likewise, the characterizations of the 1974 film generally mirror those of the 1965 movie, with different flourishes brought by each actor's performance. For example, the role originally filled by Emily Brent is once again a glamorous actress, and the ethnicities of the characters reflect the backgrounds of the international cast. As in the 1965 film, the plot point of the military man and the actress being previously met in a war-torn area is included, though in this adaptation their brief meeting was in Saigon. The extensive fistfight between Lombard and the butler, invented for the 1965 film, is reduced to a couple of punches by Lombard in response to the butler telling them all to "go to hell," and the butler never gets a chance to return the blows after being knocked to the ground. In this film, as in the 1965 version, Vera explains that her sister's fiancé was killed by her sister, and she covered for her now-deceased sibling. As there are no extenuating circumstances mentioned, that makes Vera an accessory after the fact, which means she is not an innocent, blunting the justice in her survival. In the 1975 version, Vera's sister dies of suicide. In the 1965 version, at least, though Ann protected her sister, her sister is currently in a mental institution, indicating that she may not have been entirely responsible for her actions, and Ann's actions were in the best interests of a seriously disturbed woman. The judge's last conversation with Vera reflects the changes in the law. Instead of telling her that if she does not hang herself now, the authorities will find her guilty and hang her themselves, he tells her that if she is the only survivor, she will be locked away for the rest of her life, and death would be preferable to that.

The first two couplets are recited by Vera and Lombard at the dinner table, and the rest are played by Raven (Marston) at the piano in the lounge, getting more strident and discordant with each couplet. The other guests are clearly annoyed by the unpleasant playing, as they look at each other with expressions of annoyance and respond with relief as the rhyme reaches its end, with Lombard flashing four fingers shortly after the halfway point to reassure the others of the few rhymes remaining, and right before the final couplet Ilona (Miss Brent) tells the Judge to relax, as the song will soon be finished. After this heavily staccato rendition of the rhyme, Raven sings a much pleasanter tune, "The Old Fashioned Way," which was one of his portrayer, Charles Avanzour's standards. This additional song is a nice performance, but it stops the action cold for two minutes and adds nothing to the mystery.

A few of the couplets of the rhyme have been changed as they were in the 1965 remake, reflecting the changes in the murders. While the first murder is still cyanide in a drink, the death of Elsa Martino (Mrs. Rogers) happens as she hurries across a courtyard of ruins—reflecting the "one ran away" version of the rhyme. When she takes a moment to rest against a pillar, the killer, who was either able to keep up with her without her seeing him, or else knew precisely where she would stop running and hid behind the exact pillar where she tried to catch her breath, whips a rope around both the pillar and her neck, strangling her. As she does not die in bed, this explains the change in the rhyme, though it is not clear where she was running *to* in the middle of the night. This scene spoils the mystery a bit, as three characters are cleared of suspicion. Martino (Rogers), Lombard, and Vera all see Elsa running amongst the ruins, and they hurry over to her together, arriving seconds after the murder. Lombard comments that this is "the way the ancient Persians used to execute a murderess" as he removes the rope from the body and tosses it aside. It is unclear how the murderer was able to slip away without being seen by them. In any case, as none of the three could have committed the crime, the observant viewer knows that none of them can be the murderer.

The 1965 version avoided the early exoneration of the trio, as while the three of them watched the unfortunate housekeeper die in the falling funicular, the cable had been heavily frayed before they arrived, so theoretically any of them could have damaged the cord earlier, and therefore all of them remained under suspicion. Having the housekeeper strangled changes the dynamic a little as well. Traditionally, after the first two murders, the guests are still able to soothe themselves with the possibility that there is not a killer on the loose, and that the first death was a suicide and the second was an accident or natural death. But with a rope around the victim's death, it is immediately obvious that this is the work of a multiple murderer.

The General's death occurs in the middle of an area filled with arches and mosaics, and the viewer sees the shadow of a hand holding a knife, stabbing twice. There seems to be no connection with Heaven or pussycats, which is the phrasing of the rhyme reused in this film.

Martino (Rogers') death is particularly confounding. With no phone or radio, he decides to walk two hundred miles across the desert on his own. Unfortunately for him, after he is too far on his journey to come back, he discovers that his canteen is empty and his compass has been smashed. (Why he did not check his canteen and compass before he left is not explained, nor is it explained how a single canteen was supposed to be enough water for a two-hundred-mile hike in the blazing sun.) No connection between chopping sticks or a chopper is made, unless the "chopper" is what broke his compass. He dies in the desert amongst more archaeological ruins. The viewer sees his presumably dead body splayed out on the ground, but the characters in the film never find his corpse, so by rights they should all be wondering if he is alive and hiding. Instead, they assume he is dead once Lombard finds the broken figurine. The judge suggests that it could be a trick, but the others pooh-pooh this eminently reasonable hypothesis.

Ilona (Miss Brent's) death occurs after she explains how her coldness towards her husband led him to commit suicide, as she was a woman without a country, the child of Russian refugees who wound up singing in nightclubs, who married a man just to get a passport, and he blew his head off after she revealed her indifference towards him. She goes up to her room, thinking she will be safe in privacy, but as the door opens, one wonders why she did not have the foresight to lock it (unless the killer had a key) and barricade the door as well. There is a bit of a missed opportunity, as in her last moments, she is shown hugging a teddy bear. Viewers might suspect that the bear might be connected to the death of the eighth victim, but it is not seen again.

Soon afterwards, Armstrong examines her dead body, while Wargrave stands off to the side. Vera screams when she sees the cause of death– a poisonous snake– and Lombard, ever the man of action, leaps forward, grabs a metal goblet, and beats the snake to death, declaring, "there's your bumblebee." The snake is just feet away from the kneeling Armstrong, and one wonders why the killer did not say anything, as the snake was in his line of sight and had the serpent attacked the doctor, a second death by snakebite would not fit the rhyme, although it is possible the snake used up all its venom on Ilona. The logistics of how the killer managed to either catch a snake or bring it to the hotel, and release it without getting bitten himself, are not explained, nor is any thought given to the fact that the snake could very easily have slithered away and attacked again without warning had Lombard not slain it.

Wargrave's initial "death" has him "shot" in his bedroom, but no judge's wig and robe are added to his body. The judge and the doctor made a bit of a mistake, firing Lombard's gun in the lounge and leaving it there. Even with all the chaos in the darkness after Vera's scream, it hardly makes sense that the killer would have shot the judge in the lounge and then carried his body up to his room, or lured the judge to his room, shot him there, and then brought the gun back to the lounge and abandoned it. Presumably, the judge lay down on his bed to save the others the trouble of carrying his "corpse" to his room and possibly discovering he was actually alive.

Doctor Armstrong is found dead amongst some ruins, but no explanation is made as to how he died. Blore dies from being shoved off a high balcony, but no attempt is made to link the death to a zoo or a bear. After Vera and Lombard find Armstrong's body, Lombard is amazingly calm as he talks to Vera and explains he is just impersonating the real Lombard, and is still and stoic as she points the gun at him. Due to the way the scene is cut, it is not clear as to whether Lombard convinced Vera to fire the gun away from him to draw out the real killer, or if Vera really tried to shoot him and missed completely. There is no conversation between the pair after Wargrave's confession and suicide, nor is there any confirmation of romantic feelings between them, so the viewer never knows exactly what happened between them or where their relationship might go from there.[2]

One mystery that may strike the observant viewer early in the film is that twelve actors are listed in the opening credits, for "with Teresa Gimpera and Rick Battaglia" rounds out the opening cast list. By the end of the film, the viewers who counted the names and paid close attention are quite justified in scratching their heads, as only the ten standard characters appear on-screen. Gimpera and Battaglia do not appear in the final credits, which feature a replay of Welles' recorded accusations.

The answer to these confusing credits lies in the fact that some subplots involving spies and detectives were added to the movie. As the interiors were filmed in Iran and other portions of the movie were shot in Spain, some Iranian and Spanish actors were given roles, supposedly to earn more tax credits or for other considerations to help the international production. Gimpera and Battaglia were given a handful of scenes, inserted here and there throughout the movie. The scenes were designed to be extraneous, and were probably never meant to be included in the English-language version. These scenes are totally absent from the English-language release, but they appear in the Spanish-language cut, adding about ten minutes to the run time.

These scenes have never been included in the English-language releases of the film, but they can be seen in the Spanish-language version. This version has a new opening scene, with the main characters arriving at an airport, with additional narration. A couple of new characters meet and embrace while the hotel-bound guests board a helicopter. After the new characters drive away, there are totally different actor credits, using a different font and order from what's used in the English-language version. At about twelve and fourteen minutes into the movie, there are additional scenes set at a hotel, and another scene at the film's midpoint. An additional five-second clip of an approaching helicopter is added right after Vera "shoots" Lombard, and the movie ends with a freeze frame of the dying judge, deleting some shots that close out the English-language version. There are no end credits, just "Fin."[3]

The closing credits of the English-language version of the film raise some more questions. The actors' names are arranged "in order of their disappearance," but they actually do not follow their professed order, as Ilona (Miss Brent) is listed before Martino (Rogers). Blore is listed before Dr. Armstrong, which at least makes some sense, since Blore's body is discovered before Armstrong's. But Vera Clyde's name comes before Hugh Lombard, which does not fit, as Lombard's supposed death occurred before Vera even saw the dangling noose, and Vera and Lombard appear together in their final shot.

The accusing record is replayed over the closing credits, and just as the 1965 version had a famous voice in Christopher Lee as the accusing record, this film features Orson Welles accusing all of the characters of murder.

This version only spent a brief time in theaters in the UK and received a general critical drubbing, though it received a more successful response elsewhere in Europe. There are numerous unverified rumors suggesting that some of the film's marketing and release schedule were affected by Towers' complex tax situation and studio concerns that *Ten Little Indians* might encroach upon the release of *Murder on the Orient Express* in the same year. Some members of the cast quipped that their main interest in the film was their salaries. Richard Attenborough is widely thought to have accepted his role to help fund his future film, *Gandhi*.[4] Despite the mixed reaction to the movie, Towers decided to revisit the story one more time, fifteen years later.

[1] *The Internet Movie Database*, accessed July 5, 2025, https://www.imdb.co m/title/tt0072263/?ref_=nv_sr_srsg_3_tt_8_nm_0_in_0_q_ten%2520littl e%2520indians.

[2] *Ten Little Indians*, directed by Peter Collinson, Filibuster Films/COME-CI/Coralta Cinematografica, 1974, 1hr. 38 min., (Scorpion Releasing, 2017), Blu-Ray & DVD.

[3] *Diez Negritos,* directed by Peter Collinson, Filibuster Films/COMECI/-Coralta Cinematografica, 1974, 1hr. 48 min., (Divisa), DVD/Blu-Ray.

[4] *"Ten Little Indians* (1974)."

Chapter Twenty-Eight

Desyat Negrityat (1987 Russian Feature Film)

Tatyana Drubich: Vera Elizabeth Claythorne
Aleksandr Kaydanovskiy: Captain Philip Lombard
Aleksey Zharkov: William Henry Blore
Anatoli Romashin: Dr. Edward George Armstrong
Vladimir Zeldin: Judge Lawrence John Wargrave
Lyudmila Maksakova: Emily Caroline Brent
Aleksey Zolotnitskiy: Thomas Rogers
Mikhail Gluzskiy: General John Gordon Macarthur
Irina Tereshchenko: Ethel Rogers
Aleksandr Abdulov: Anthony James Marston
Viktor Bentsler: Vera's fiancé
Fyodor Odinokov (as F. Odinokov): Fred Narracott
Directed by Stanislav Govorukhin
Screenplay by Stanislav Govorukhin[1]

esyat Negrityat is one of, if not *the* most faithful, film adaptations of *And Then There Were None* yet. Aside from a few minor changes, this Russian production largely matches the novel scene for scene, and if the subtitles are a reliable translation, the dialogue is often taken nearly verbatim from Christie's book, aside from a couple of comments from Emily Brent, which are borrowed from Mrs. Boyle's lines in *The*

Mousetrap. Reflecting the fidelity to the original story, the names are all the same, the deaths they caused in the past are unaltered, the means of murder are unchanged, and the atmosphere is dark and suspenseful, with few moments of levity. The title translates to the original name of the book, and the ten figurines are each slightly different and are caricaturized statuettes of Black people.

Extremely observant viewers will catch a quick scene that gives away the identity of the killer early on in the movie. Moments before Marston's death, there is a shot from overhead that includes most of the suspects (save for Mrs. Rogers, who has already been taken to her room). Off to one side of the screen, Wargrave quickly flicks his wrist over Marston's glass, presumably adding the cyanide that Marston drinks soon afterwards. His death is rather more gruesome than in the book, as he collapses on the table, breaking a glass and leaving shards in his face. A copious amount of blood flows from the lacerations.

For a few brief moments, strict realism gives way to hallucination, such as when Emily Brent imagines that she sees Beatrice Taylor pounding on her bedroom window, begging to be let inside the house.

There is one major deviation from the source material. During their last night alive, a frightened Vera bursts into Lombard's room. While in the 1960s version, their late-night encounter appeared to be wholly consensual, in *Desyat Negrityat*, Lombard seems to force himself upon Vera after her initial protests, and he callously snaps that she ought not to have come to his room in her nightclothes if she had not expected that to happen. This assault, coupled with Vera's facial expressions, adds additional implications to the scene where she shoots him on the beach.

The ending is a bit different from any other version. After shooting Lombard and returning to the house, Vera is in a sort of fugue state. She passes by the open door of Wargrave's bedroom, where his presumed corpse is lying on the bed. Moments after she walks away, Wargrave is shown stirring and rising. He is not dressed in a makeshift judicial outfit made from a shower curtain and yarn, but instead is wearing his actual official robes (they must have been hidden, so no one saw them and questioned why he packed them for a weekend visit) and an academic mortarboard. He enters Vera's bedroom moments after she hangs herself, and the closing moments of the film feature him mentally explaining his crimes and his reasons for going outside the law. In one of the few instances of original dialogue, he applauds Vera for realizing that she deserved to die and taking care of her own execution, and declares that he will do the same. He burns his robes in the fireplace, and the final moments of the film see him raising the gun to his head, and the camera pans around the back of his chair before the sound of a shot. The chair obscures the judge's body.

This movie led the contemporary trend of keeping to the original dark ending and tone, and is ultimately one of the most faithful Christie adaptations ever filmed.[2]

[1] *"Ten Little Indians* (Original title: *Desyat negrityat*), (1987)," *The Internet Movie Database*, accessed July 5, 2025, https://www.imdb.com/title/tt0092 879/?ref_=ttfc_ov_bk.

[2] *Desyat Negrityat*, directed by Stanislav Govorukhin, Odessa Film Studio, 1987, 2 hrs. 17 min., DVD.

Chapter Twenty-Nine

Ten Little Indians (1989 Feature Film)

Sarah Maur Ward (as Sarah Maur Thorp): Vera Claythorne
Frank Stallone: Captain Lombard
Warren Berlinger: Mr. Blore
Yehuda Efroni: Dr. Werner (Armstrong)
Donald Pleasence: Judge Wargrave
Brenda Vaccaro: Marion Marshall (Brent)
Paul L. Smith: Mr. Rodgers (sic)
Herbert Lom: General Romensky (Macarthur)
Moria Lister: Mrs. Rodgers (sic)
Neil McCarthy: Anthony Marston
Directed by Alan Birkinshaw
Screenplay by Jackson Hunsicker and Gerry O'Hara[1]

Of the three Harry Alan Towers remakes, the 1989 version is last and least. While the 1974 version was denigrated by critics, the 1989 version is generally held in even lower esteem.

This version transfers the action to a safari in an isolated region of Africa. Instead of being ferried to their destination, six of the characters take the train and are dropped off alongside the tracks in the middle of the savannah. They are greeted by Lombard, who is to be their tour guide on safari. A group of Africans who communicate through clicking noises carry their baggage (as well as the character of Marion Marshall, again an actress, though this time a middle-aged one, replacing Miss Brent, the only guest to be carried in a sedan chair). A small plane drops off Marston before flying away again, and the party, now totaling eight guests and the Africans, make their way to a ravine, where they pull themselves down using a rickety manual funicular consisting of frayed ropes and a fragile-looking basket. Moments after the last of them have successfully descended, one of the Africans atop the cliff pulls out a knife and slashes a rope, causing the funicular to smash against the side of the ravine, leaving the guests on their own.

After a short hike, the eight guests arrive at a campsite, filled with already set-up tents. Mr. and Mrs. Rodgers (a "d" has been inserted into their name, and Mr. Rodgers has been given the first name "Elmo") are Americans who have won a free trip to Africa. They are not the hired help, but they arrived at the campsite a day before everybody else, and Mr. Rodgers has taken it upon himself to do all the cooking.

Upon arrival, Lombard checks the radio and discovers that it is working, but he does not do the sensible thing and call for help immediately. Instead, he simply confirms that it works, and then is shocked a little while later when the radio has been broken during his absence. He is able to fix it reasonably quickly, and late in the film, he calls for a rescue plane, though had he called for help immediately, several lives might have been saved.

For the most part, the remainder of the movie follows the standard plot, with the guests dying in the expected order. When half the guests are dead, there is a massive rainstorm, but there is no scene where Blore messes up and breaks the generator, leaving them without power. The ending adds a bit more violence to the face-off between Vera and Wargrave. Wargrave dresses in his scarlet judge's robes and wig, not bothering to wipe away the tomato sauce from his forehead. He forces Vera into a noose at gunpoint, and yanks out the chair from under her. Vera manages to hoist herself up by clinging to the rope above her head, and Wargrave chuckles, thinking she will not be able to hold on for very long before she lets go and strangles. He succumbs to the hemlock-laced wine he drank a few moments earlier, but unlike most of the movies, during his last seconds, he does not see that

Lombard is still alive and able to spoil his plan for committing unsolvable murders. Lombard survives his skirmish with Vera without serious injury, but they did not work together to fake the shooting– as in the play, Vera could not shoot straight, and the bullet appears to have completely missed him. Lombard frees Vera from the noose, and they hurry out to meet the rescue plane that just landed.

Many of the characters are radically different from earlier versions. Marston is an empty-headed British foppish sort, not too far off from the original novel, but while other film versions portrayed his character as having substantial musical skills, this version of Marston's talent is much more limited, as he only knows a few lines of "Wild Dogs and Englishmen." In this version, he freely confesses to the vehicular double homicide and shows no remorse, but whereas in the book the law briefly suspended his license, in this version, his father confiscated his car.

The Mrs. Rodgers in this film is a garrulous woman with no interest in domestic work, a far cry from the "bloodless" housekeeper of the novel. She is friendly to Vera, and she sits with the eight guests during her only meal at the dinner table, while her husband keeps to the kitchen. They are from the American Midwest and were told they had won the safari vacation in a contest. Otherwise, her limited screen time and actions are relatively close to the original source material, as she freaks out after the accusatory record.

The General (renamed Romensky) is from the Balkans, and portrayed by Herbert Lom, who played the doctor in the 1974 film). The character is quite similar to the original source material, with a brusque military manner. Here, his mental decline appears more obvious at times. When the other men remove Marston's body, the General leads but does not lift, counting to three before intending to tell them to pick up the corpse, though he mistakenly says "fire!," throwing off everybody. Later, he mistakes Vera for his late wife.

Elmo Rodgers is a huge mountain of a man. Other than volunteering his culinary skills, he spends his time glowering and physically intimidating the others without touching them.

The American Marion Marshall is a sharp departure from both the original

Emily Brent and the previous two remakes, which turned the character into a glamorous younger actress near the peak of her career. Here, she has had a film career at least a couple of decades long, and she is famous enough for Vera to know a lot about her past, but apparently, she is not sufficiently popular for the characters to fawn over her. She is also demonstrative in her emotions and easily flustered. Unlike the secular actresses in the previous Towers remakes, Marshall is a religious woman, praying multiple times, putting her faith in the Lord to protect her, and reading her pocket Bible. She carries more than the Good Book around with her, for she possesses a flask as well, as does the doctor. One large difference is that the woman Marshall's accused of killing is another Hollywood actress whose star was on the decline. Ostensibly, she and Marshall were close friends, but in reality, the two were having a lesbian relationship that soured. When her angry, soon-to-be-ex-partner threatened to tell the world about their affair, the two fought, and the other woman drowned in her pool.

The British judge's characterization is reasonably close to the original, having a similar personality and role. There is a brief moment of potential character inconsistency when, after all the travelers have descended down into the ravine and the Africans destroy the funicular, Wargrave abruptly becomes frantic for a few seconds, declaring that he knew something was up, as he claims to "know natives." As he no doubt arranged for them to slash the rope to the funicular, he was not surprised, so his brief histrionics must be acting. Perhaps the point of this uncharacteristic display was to rattle the others. Aside from the fact that this version of Wargrave is a widower, there is not much difference from the novel's judge.

The medical man's name has been changed to Dr. Werner, and as the actor Yehuda Efroni is Israeli, it seems that the character, who speaks with an accent, shares that background. Otherwise, there are not many sharp changes to his characterization.

This Blore is an American ex-cop who sent a guilty old friend to prison for burglary. When the imprisoned man intended to provide information to the police, Blore implies that he had him killed in jail, but it is not clear how he did it. Blore is a formidably-sized man, though Rodgers dwarfs him, and he intends to defend himself with the guns found at the camp, and is profanely enraged when all of the ammunition proves to be blanks.

Captain Lombard is also from the United States, and his role and characterizations are reasonably close to the earlier versions, and the same can be said for the British Vera.

A few of the deaths have been changed. The General is killed by being pushed down a rocky slope. An arm with a rolled-up sleeve is shown shoving him in the back, and the sharp-eyed viewer can tell it is a man's hand, which automatically eliminates the two women as suspects. There is a bit of a red herring, as while a couple of characters have their sleeves rolled up, the killer must have removed his jacket and rolled up his shirtsleeves before the fatal push. From the perspective of the film's characters, who, apart from the killer, did not see it happen, the general could have fallen accidentally, so the question of whether the deaths are murders is not confirmed until Elmo Rodgers gets a hatchet to the back of the head. Unlike the 1945 adaptation, which took a "tell, don't show" approach to this grisly death, Elmo Rodgers' murder wound is filmed in all its grisly glory in multiple shots. Rodgers decided not to sleep that night, so he climbed up a hill to keep an eye on the others as they slept. It is not explained how the killer managed to sneak out of his tent and creep up the hill without being seen by Rodgers, though it is possible Rodgers may have been drugged at dinner, allowing the killer to approach him undetected.

With no natural source of water nearby, Doctor Werner is not drowned, but instead is killed in an unspecified way (possibly a stab wound to the throat, the camera does not linger long enough to make the details clear) that caused a smallish amount of blood to be spilt, and the body is tucked inside a large, zippered pouch, possibly containing water. With no mystery over what happened to the Doctor, Vera, Lombard, and Blore immediately suspect each other. The sensible thing to do would be for the three to keep an eye on each other, but Vera runs off screaming, hysterically declaring she won't stay around the two men, and Lombard and Blore decide to split up as well.

This proves to be fatal for Blore. Marston carried a little teddy bear in his flight suit as a good luck charm. The teddy bear is then punctured with a long knife, which is then used to stab Blore.

The viewer who is unfamiliar with the story would never anticipate that the bear would have anything to do with the eighth death. The entire rhyme is never shown on-screen, nor is the rhyme sung early in the movie. The first two couplets are recited at the dinner scene, but the other couplets are mostly only stated shortly before or even after the deaths, so the unfamiliar viewer often has no idea what kind of murders to anticipate. The phrasing of the song is a little different in places from the traditional wording, and some of the couplets are incompletely spoken. The second-to-last couplet is not mentioned at all.

While most of the remakes were set roughly contemporaneously to their filming, this version must be set right around 1939, the year of the book's publication, based on the fact that years of death are mentioned on the phonograph record, and references to how much time has passed, the movie has to occur during the late 1930s, probably before the outbreak of the Second World War.

Aside from a bit more gore, there's also a few brief outbursts of profanity, There is no hint of sex between Vera and Lombard—the closest they get to romance is Vera's quick peck on Lombard's cheek, and the most physical contact they have is when they tumble to the ground fighting over the gun, and when Lombard holds Vera up to prevent her from strangling in the noose.

The ten figurines are small dark wooden African men (imitations of actual African art, according to Marshall), and each death sees a head broken off a doll. They appear too top-heavy to stand up, and are arranged in a shallow wooden dish which is made of the same material as the figurines, which, even in close-ups, makes it hard to tell sometimes how many statuettes have been decapitated. A lighter tray would have made it much easier to see the damage. Aside from the last doll, whose head is broken off on-camera, it is never shown what happened to the little wooden heads. Before the fourth murder, the doctor gets the idea to thwart U.N. Owen by locking away the remaining wooden figures and giving Rodgers the key. However, he locks them away in a cabinet with an extremely fragile glass door, so even if the killer had not retrieved the key, it would have been easy for him to break the glass and take the figurines.

The pacing of the movie is a bit uneven. In approximately one hundred minutes of run time, the deaths do not start until half an hour in, and the last three deaths and two non-deaths happen in rapid succession, starting twenty minutes before the movie's end.

There are a few technical mistakes. The actress Marion Marshall is American, but the screenwriters may not have known that an actress from the United States would be cast in the role, because she refers to getting a letter "in the post," when an American would say "in the mail." At dinner, Marston seems surprised and delighted to learn that there is a piano, but he was in the communal gathering tent earlier, so he should have seen it. A piano is, after all, rather large and hard to miss. Marston's last drink is a glass of champagne, and as he starts choking, he drops the glass off-screen, and there is a sound of smashing. Yet when the doctor and Blore retrieve the glass later and examine it, there is not so much as a chip in it. One seeming error is just a character being unobservant. After Marston is buried, Marion Marshall states that they never learned his first name. They did, actually, as Marston's first and middle names are mentioned in the record, but Marshall's portrayed as being a bit scatterbrained, so it is perfectly in-character for her not to have paid attention to this.

In the credits, Donald Pleasance and Brenda Vaccaro get top billing. Moira Lister is next to last, and she gets a "with" before her name, as well as a "as Mrs. Rodgers" in her opening credit, followed by "and Paul Smith," though his role as Mr. Rodgers is not named. The closing credits, showing brief video clips of the characters, is in much the same order as the opening credits, to the tune of "Wild Dogs and Englishmen."

The opening credits state that the film is based on Christie's play, not her novel, though there are a number of cases where the screenplay draws upon previous versions of the film rather than anything written by Christie. Starting in the 1945 movie, the judge and the doctor have shared a scene at a billiard table. In the middle of the savannah, the pair's conversation instead revolves around a game of croquet. Likewise, the 1945 addition of the seven still-alive guests voting on the most likely suspect after the third murder, with Vera getting no votes and Rodgers (however it is spelled in the adaptation) getting two, is also included after being absent in the 1965 and 1974 adaptations. The 1945 addition of another guest to the island—a pet cat who survived the carnage—is given a different riff here. Here, there is a tame monkey who jumps around the guests and steals Marston's cigarette, but the primate plays no role in the movie aside from some brief early scenes. There is also a lioness stalking the campsite, but she plays no important role in the plot. "Lombard" is actually an innocent man who took over his dead friend—the real Lombard's—identity but kept his own suitcase with his own initials, just like in the 1945 movie.[2]

To date, there has not been another English-language feature film remake of *And Then There Were None*, though anything is possible in the future.

[1] *"Ten Little Indians* (1989)," *The Internet Movie Database*, accessed July 5, 2025, https://www.imdb.com/title/tt0098454/?ref_=fn_all_ttl_2.

[2] *Ten Little Indians*, directed by Alan Birkinshaw, Breton Film Productions/Pathe Communications, 1989, 1 hr. 40 min., (KI Studio Classics, 2020), DVD.

Chapter Thirty

And Then There Were None (2015 BBC Television Miniseries)

Maeve Dermody: Vera Claythorne
Aidan Turner: Philip Lombard
Burn Forman: Detective Sergeant William Blore
Toby Stephens: Doctor Edward Armstrong
Charles Dance: Judge Lawrence Wargrave
Miranda Richardson: Emily Brent
Noah Taylor: Thomas Rogers
Sam Neill: General John MacArthur
Anna Maxwell Martin: Ethel Rogers
Douglas Booth: Anthony Marston
Christopher Hatherall: Fred Narracott
Rob Heaps: Hugo
Harley Gallacher: Cyril Oglivie Hamilton
Paul Chahidi: Isaac Morris
Directed by Craig Viveiros
Screenplay by Sarah Phelps[1]

In the DVD special features for the 2015 miniseries, released around Christie's 125th birthday, multiple people connected to the production state that this is the first time that the novel has ever been adapted for television, when in fact there were several television productions of *And*

Then There Were None over the decades. The 2015 BBC version, however, was the first English-language official adaptation to use the novel's ending, rather than the play's. The three-part production was composed of hour-long episodes.

Each episode (after the "previously on" segments for episodes two and three) begins with a credits scene featuring ten green statuettes made of jade or some similar stone material, all in an abstract human form, though the postures are different for each figurine. Words from the nursery rhyme are superimposed on the statuettes, and one by one they crumble, and the pieces of green stone join together to form the mansion and island in the credits' closing moments. In episode one, all ten main actors are included in the credits, but once a character dies, the actor's name is removed. Episode two's credits feature eight names, and episode three lists only five.

The general narrative remains very close to the book, though some aspects regarding the characters' crimes and their murders have been altered. Some of the characters' crimes have been changed from being unprovable murders to acts of violence that really should have been caught by the authorities. Rogers, in this adaptation, rather than neglecting to administer medicine, places a pillow over his employer's face in a flashback, while a terrified Mrs. Rogers watches the smothering from the other side of the room, and proclaims them both damned afterwards. General MacArthur (bringing back the original name, albeit with a capitalized "A") shoots his wife's lover instead of sending him off on a fatal mission, and it is unclear what happened next– could the body have been staged to look like it was hit by an enemy's bullet on the battlefield? It is not clear. Emily Brent is implied to have had lesbian feelings towards her unfortunate young maid. Blore, instead of perjuring himself, gay-bashes a young man to a pulp in a prison cell, and it is not spelled out why he did not face consequences for his actions. Lombard's crime is largely the same as what it was before, only the motive in this case is diamonds rather than simple survival. Hugo is turned into a much stronger character, as he realizes that the athletic Vera could easily have caught up with little Cyril, and he accuses her of murder, though he regrets that he cannot prove her guilt.

The deaths of the characters are mostly changed in small ways. Marston's death is a bit grislier, as he coughs up blood all over Vera after downing the poison. The means by which the poison is administered to Mrs. Rogers is not clarified, and a scene where an unseen person visits a still-awake Mrs. Rogers in her bedroom indicates that someone administered a fatal dose to her during that visit, somehow. While the blunt instrument that killed MacArthur is never identified in the book, the General is bludgeoned with his own telescope in this adaptation. Rather than a single blow to the head with an axe, Rogers is practically disemboweled with an axe here, and Lombard and Blore have a gory time moving the body and cleaning up the mess. Emily Brent is not killed with a hypodermic, but instead is stabbed in the throat with one of her own knitting needles, which has a "B" engraved on it. Wargrave's faked death now includes some liver and kidneys taken from the pantry for added verisimilitude, as the offal is used to simulate brain matter. Blore is not killed by a falling clock shaped like a bear, but instead is stabbed with a kitchen knife while the killer wears a bearskin rug. Armstrong's, Lombard's, and Vera's deaths remain essentially the same, though Wargrave walks in on Vera as she hangs herself, and he explains his actions—though not how he found out about his victims' past crimes, as she precariously balances on the back of the kicked-over chair. Wargrave moves the chair away once he is done talking and Vera has inadvertently confessed to Cyril's death, though he does not wipe his prints from the chair, thereby leaving an incriminating clue behind him. Immediately after Vera's death, Wargrave adjourns to the dining room dressed in his suit (nothing resembling judge's robes, though the gray wool and scarlet curtain were used to fake his death), pours himself some wine, and sips it, not bothering to finish the glass. He then shoots himself under the chin with his hands protected by a napkin, and after the shot is fired, the gun flies out of his hands, and the recoil carries the gun to the other end of the table as if by magic, making it look like some other person left it there after the shooting.

While Wargrave does not explain how he learned about the others' crimes, there are blink-and-you-will-miss-them references throughout the series that suggest how these suspicions reached him. Marston's crime was on record, and Rogers suggests that there was gossip amongst the other servants. A nurse's voice in a flashback scene suggests she later talked about the doctor's drunkenness, Blore's co-workers may have said something, Lombard notes that he had accomplices whose consciences may have bothered him when they were safely home, and Hugo may have voiced his certainty of Vera's murderousness.

Isaac Morris makes his screen debut in this adaptation and is shown recruiting Lombard and Vera, but there is no indication that he was killed.

While the plot remains the same, most of the dialogue is created freshly for the show, often providing additional character details with notable changes. Emily Brent, for example, has her attitudes on class played up in a new scene with Mrs. Rogers; the anti-Semitic attitudes previously embodied by Lombard are now imposed on her, and the gaps in her historical knowledge are shown when she considers "Norman" to be a quintessentially British name.

The adaptation features a lot more adult content than previous entries. Aside from frequent swearing, sex scenes between Vera and Lombard, as well as Vera and Hugo, are shown on-screen. Marston sniffs cocaine, and late in the series, Vera, Lombard, Blore, and Armstrong snort the remaining drugs and also get drunk in a bacchanal. Blood and gore are also present, as Blore and Lombard get soaked in Rogers' bodily fluids as they move the body and clean up the crime scene.

Some of the changes produce minor plot holes. The revolver is not hidden in a tin of biscuits as in the book, but instead is stuffed into the mouth of the bearskin rug, alongside the master key to the mansion. It is unclear why the killer believed that no one would discover these items there, where they would be in plain sight by anybody who got down on their hands and knees to search. Additionally, the ten statuettes disappear and are not broken, and all ten are replaced in their original spot at the production's end. It is not revealed where Wargrave hid the statuettes so that they would not be discovered during the search.

Another change that does not affect the plot includes Armstrong being slapped by Vera when he gets hysterical, rather than the other way around, serving as a poke in the eye for his earlier, frequent misogynistic comments towards Vera.

There are a few new clues. When the accusatory record is played, Wargrave looks at Blore when the latter's name is called, even though the judge supposedly only knew him as "Davis" at this time. Wargrave plays up how frail and weak he is in an early scene, claiming he cannot carry his own suitcase, and welcomes assistance climbing the stairs. Yet later on, when a distraught Vera attempts to swim to the mainland, a surprisingly vigorous Wargrave wades out into the sea after her and pulls her back to land. While all of the other characters are shown to be definitely guilty in flashbacks, Wargrave's flashbacks indicate that Seton was indeed a multiple murderer, showing that Wargrave is the only one who did not commit a murder in the past, as the death sentence he passed was within the strictures of the law.[2]

Richard Hope (who also played Superintendent Spence in two episodes of the David Suchet series *Agatha Christie's Poirot*) was cast as Inspector Maine, the detective who investigates the case in the penultimate chapter and concludes that none of the people on the island could have done it, but his scene was deleted before broadcast.

This was the first of several Christie adaptations written by Sarah Phelps, followed by *Witness for the Prosecution* (based on the short story, not the play), *Ordeal by Innocence*, *The ABC Murders*, and *The Pale Horse*.[3] While *And Then There Were None* was known for its general closeness to the original story, though almost none of the original dialogue remained, her later adaptations made major changes, such as altering the killer's identity, providing a backstory for Poirot absent from the original canon, changing main characters' personalities and fates, and adding much more sex, profanity, on-screen calls of nature, and crudeness.[4]

[1] "*And Then There Were None* (2015)," *The Internet Movie Database*, accessed July 5, 2025, https://www.imdb.com/title/tt3581932/?ref_=nv_sr_srsg_0_tt_8_nm_0_in_0_q_and%2520then%2520there.

[2] *And Then There Were None*, directed by Craig Viveiros, Mammoth

Screen/Agatha Christie Productions/BBC, 2015, 2 hrs. 54 min., (Acorn Media, 2016), DVD.

[3] A Phelps-scripted adaptation of *Endless Night* is in development as of this writing.

[4] "*And Then There Were None* (2015)."

Chapter Thirty-One

Japanese Version: Soshite daremo inakunatta (2017)

Yukie Nakama: Shiramine Ryô (Claythorne)
Yoshiyoshi Arakawa: Banpei Tartara (Lombard)
Jun Kunimura: Kumabe Kenkichi (Blore)
Kimiko Yo: Dr. Kônami Erika (Armstrong)
Tsunehiko Watase: Iwamura Hyogo (Wargrave)
Mao Daichi: Miss Hoshizora Ayako (Brent)
Isao Hashizume: Mr Midorikawa (Mr. Rogers)
Toshirô Yanagiba: Ken Ishirugi (Macarthur)
Mariko Fuji: Mrs. Midorikawa (Mrs. Rogers)
Osamu Mukai: Gomyo Taku (Marston)
Masahiko Tsugawa: Monden Senmei (Police Detective)
Directed by Akiyoshi Kimata
Screenplay by Shûkei Nagasaka[1]

Starting in 2015, several Christie novels were given Japanese adaptations, transferring the action to Japan and casting Japanese actors. Some, like 2015's adaptation of *Murder on the Orient Express*, were both very faithful and greatly expanded the work. The first half of the *Murder on the Orient Express* adaptation mirrored the book closely. The second half was a largely original narrative exploring the backstory of all of the characters.

This 2017 two-part television adaptation of *And Then There Were None* is largely very close to the original adaptation, but it makes some significant changes and adjustments. It is set in present-day Japan, and most of the events are told in flashback, as a team of police officers travel to the island to investigate the murders, but it is the lead police officer who observes the important clues and makes the correct deductions, piecing the puzzle together largely by himself. In this version, the characters are invited to a hotel that encourages the guests to get back to nature, so all cell phones and electronic devices are confiscated upon their arrival, and newspapers are delivered to the island by drone. Like the original book, all ten characters on the island die.

A few of the characters have been substantially changed. The equivalents of Mr. and Mrs. Rogers, Wargrave, Blore, and Vera are very close to the originals. The Marston equivalent is by far the most changed, as he is friendlier, smarter, and nicer than any of the other Marstons. He is an ex-boxer turned mystery writer, and he and Vera seem to have a connection before his untimely death. The Macarthur equivalent is very similar to the novel's version, but he seems to have escaped senility. He is fairly mentally sharp, and even does card tricks where one card levitates. He now holds a prominent position in the government. The Emily Brent equivalent has once again been turned into a glamorous actress, though of slightly more mature years than in the 1965 and 1974 versions. The doctor has been given a gender swap, but her basic personality and backstory are not too different from the original character. The Lombard equivalent is older, gruffer, and does not seem to be romantically interested in Vera, nor she in him.

Most of the crimes the characters committed have been radically altered. The Marston equivalent thought he was witnessing a crime and mistakenly punched an innocent man, believing him to be threatening a woman. As a trained boxer, his blows inadvertently proved fatal, and as the authorities believed his intentions were good, he received a slap on the wrist. This killing would likely be ruled an involuntary manslaughter by American standards, and the actor's facial expressions indicates that he is deeply remorseful for what happened. The Rogers equivalents do not withhold medication from their employer, but instead, the butler smothers his boss as she lies helpless in a hospital bed, while the housekeeper looks on, clearly distraught but refusing to stop her husband. The Macarthur equivalent discovers his wife is having an affair with his aide, and lures the man to a building where he has advance warning that a terrorist attack will occur. His wife's lover is then killed by a bomb.

The Emily Brent equivalent has a close relationship with her maid, and is shown letting the girl try on her jewelry, though it is a bit ambiguous as to whether the actress's feelings are maternal or romantic. In any event, the maid becomes pregnant by an unknown man, but unlike the book, the Brent equivalent takes her maid to the hospital, ostensibly to give her a checkup. Unbeknownst to the maid, the actress convinces the doctor to give the maid an abortion, insisting she is too young to become a mother. When the maid realizes what happened against her will, she is devastated and commits suicide.

The deaths that the judge, the doctor, and the Blore equivalent are accused of are very close to the book. The Blore equivalent perjured himself to get his lover's spouse out of the way. The Lombard equivalent is a mercenary who causes multiple deaths to save himself and his daughter. The Vera equivalent is a former professional swimmer turned tutor. Her crime is very similar to the original novel, though in this case, she leaves the sickly young boy in her charge alone while she gets his heart medicine, and the boy drowns in an indoor public pool with a strong current. As a hallucination presumably based on memory shows, the Hugo equivalent knew what she had done and accuses her, though he cannot prove her guilt.

Nearly all of the murders of the people on the island are almost exactly the same as in the book, with the exception of the Blore equivalent, as he is clubbed on the head with a stone carving shaped like a bear along an outside pathway, rather than having a bear-shaped clock falling on his head from a height. When the judge "dies," he is made up to look like a judge from the Meiji period, with a blue tapestry and a fishing rod used to make the judicial robes, and a ball of grey yarn being used to create a top knot, rather than the British equivalents.

The ten soldier boy statuettes are traditional Japanese warriors, each one different from the others. They are arranged in a line under a glass case in the dining room, and one of the mysteries revolves around how the killer is able to make the statuettes disappear, as the glass case is so heavy it cannot be lifted. The lead detective realizes that the glass cover is mechanized, and a hidden switch in the wood paneling makes it rise and fall.

A new final act has been created for this adaptation, as the lead police detective figures out exactly what happened, deducing that there were hidden video cameras throughout the hotel, and uncovering tapes of what happened during those fatal days on the island. The authorities initially believe that the judge was the first to die, but the lead investigator believes that the forensic evidence is mistaken, explaining that the judge's time of death was affected by being enclosed in a room with a smoky fireplace. The judge was found in his room in a chair, covered with a sheet, with the window open. After some experimentation, the lead detective realizes that the judge shot himself with a heavy weight tied to the gun with a long piece of seaweed. After the gun was fired, the weight, dangling out the window, carried the gun out to the ground below. The mice infesting the island ate up the seaweed. Prior to shooting himself, the judge attached two corners of a sheet to the ceiling with wax. Soon after he died, the heat of the fireplace melted the wax, causing the sheet to drop down and cover him.

The closing scene consists of the judge's confession, consisting of a pre-recorded video message found on a hidden tape, where the judge confesses to all of the murders on the island before he even committed them—showing how well-planned the deaths were and how lucky the judge was, everything went as planned. Additionally, the judge's assistant in setting up the crimes, the equivalent of Isaac Morris, was also responsible for someone's death, and was killed and buried in the judge's yard. At the end of his confession, the judge boasts about how his crimes were a form of art, but it is the lead detective who has the last word, and as he sails back to the mainland with his subordinates, he muses that murder should never be considered art.[2]

[1] *"Soshite daremo inakunatta,"* *The Internet Movie Database*, accessed July 5,

2025, https://www.imdb.com/title/tt7031398/?ref_=fn_all_ttl_1.

[2] *Soshite daremo inakunatta*, directed by Akiyoshi Kimata, 2017, 3 hrs. 35 min.

Chapter Thirty-Two

Ils étaient dix (They Were Ten) (2020)

Samuel Le Bihan: Xavier Troussaud
Guillaume de Tonquédec: Gilles Delfour
Marianne Denicourt: Eve Lombardi
Romane Bohringer: Victoria Deshotel
Patrick Mille: Vincent Del Piero
Matlida Lutz: Nina Goldberg
Manon Azem: Kelly Nesib (also spelled Nessib)
Nassim Lyes: Malik Alaoui
Samy Seghir: Eddy Hamraoui
Isabelle Candelier: Myriam Berto
Mathieu Demy: Mathieu Le Goff
Samuel Jouy: Arnaud
Wendy Nieto: Léonie Baptista
Virginie Ledoyen: Barbara
Directed by Pascal Laugier
Screenplay by Bruno Dega and Jeanne Le Guillou[1]

The twenty-first century has seen many of Christie's novels being made into French-language adaptations, often with major changes. The series *Les petits meutres d'Agatha Christie* (2009-2024) adapted dozens of Christie's novels, but all of her classic detectives were absent.

French police officers and their associates investigated the cases set in the 1930s, 1950s, and 1970s, and some episodes were only loosely inspired by Christie's books.

Some of the same producers behind *Les petits meutres d'Agatha Christie* also worked on *Ils étaient dix*, a six-part adaptation of *And Then There Were None* that makes substantial alterations to the book. Each episode is about forty-five minutes. Most of the dialogue is in French, but some scenes are in English or Arabic. The action is moved to an island in the Caribbean in the present day. The ten wooden statuettes are all different and are all carved in an art form developed in that region. Like the Japanese miniseries, most of the story is technically in flashback, as two detectives, Mathieu Le Goff and Leonie Batista, come to the island and discover it nearly deserted, save for corpses.

Nearly all of the characters have been radically altered, which is why the cast list does not match the changed names with the original characters. Perhaps the closest to the source material is Nina Goldberg, who is reasonably close to Vera, aside from being a botanist. Nina's relationship with humanitarian aid worker Malik Alaoui is much like that of Vera and Lombard. The character of Eve Lombardi, a former police officer, bears no resemblance to Lombard aside from being the only one to confess her past actions openly. Eve is not particularly analogous to the ex-cop Blore, either. Many of the other characters contain bits and pieces of the original characters and their backstories, but for the most part, they are newly created for this production.

The nursery rhyme has been completely deleted, so there is no particular reason why each character is killed in a certain way, such as being stabbed or beaten or drowned. After each murder, there is a message, translating to something like "A mother's love can be deadly," or "Youth is no excuse." The messages appear on a computer screen before one guest smashes it, and after this point, messages are scrawled on various surfaces. The killer leaves various items around the hotel rooms in order to taunt the others and to remind them of their crimes, such as live fish in drawers, or a little statuette of Marilyn Monroe for the person who killed a girl named Marilyn.

The killer keeps a "villain's lair" in an underground room, filled with video cameras, allowing for total surveillance of the island, which is also peppered with booby traps, including a pit with a poisonous snake, which come close to killing characters, but fail.

Though the two detectives appear in each episode, only the ten characters on the island appear in the opening credits. Starting in episode two, after the first murder, the names of the dead characters are crossed off with a big red slash. The final image of the credits is the ten statuettes in two rows of five, with statuettes fading with each passing episode, the number corresponding to the number of deaths.

In most cases, the viewer learns about each character's crimes through flashbacks, sometimes entirely in the episode where that character dies, sometimes spread out over multiple episodes, ending in that character's death. In most cases, the other characters, not counting the murderer, never learn who the others killed. The first to die, Myriam Berto, a hotel employee, is not nearly as scared and "bloodless" as Mrs. Rogers. In her flashback scene, told right before the end of the first episode, Myriam's son rapes a young woman, who tearfully comes to Myriam for help. Myriam promises that she will turn over her son to the authorities, but changes her mind after watching her son sleep. Instead, Myriam pours water on the kitchen floor, and when her son's victim walks into the puddle, Myriam throws a live wire into the water, electrocuting the poor woman. After the flashback ends, a cloaked figure strikes Myriam on the head, and she falls into the pool.

A non-human, totally innocent victim is added in the form of Kelly Nessib's (a saleswoman) pet dog. The killer dropped a toxic plant into the water cistern, and the dog died after drinking a bowl of water. The humans know they cannot drink the water, and everybody fears they will die of thirst until a downpour provides them with much-needed hydration.

The equivalent of Isaac Morris is also found dead on the island, and the others recognize him as being pivotal to their being brought to the island, as he adopted various personas to lure them there for personal or professional reasons.

Giles Delfour is a stuffy entrepreneur who was badly bullied as a child.

He pushed his principal tormentor off a bridge onto the train tracks below and was never caught or punished. As retribution, he is stripped of all his clothing save for his underwear and tied to a bed. The hooded killer releases three scorpions, which crawl up his body, terrifying Giles in his last moments before he is fatally stung at the end of the second episode.

Eddy Hamraoui, the other hotel employee, is shown to have been entrusted with transporting migrants across the country. In an attempt to meet a deadline by his shady bosses, he drove a truck filled with immigrants for hours without stopping, but before he could complete his mission, they all died of heat in the unventilated truck. Eddy ran away and abandoned the truck. Most of the other characters suspect Eddy of the crimes on the island, and he is tied up against a tree. He escapes, but not for long, as he is stabbed in the chest by the killer midway through the third episode.

Eve Lombardi explains in the second episode that during the course of one of her investigations, a mentally ill, disheveled woman accused a charming, handsome man of sexually assaulting her. Lombardi did not believe the woman, and her assailant was set free, but he was later proven guilty when he attacked and killed another woman. Lombardi left the police force not long afterwards, never forgiving herself for her lapse of judgment. Kelly draws everybody's attention to Eve's body, floating in the sea at the end of the third episode, quickly drifting too far away for anybody to retrieve it.

Xavier Troussard is a soldier who was devastated to learn that he cannot father a child. He grows angry once his wife reveals her pregnancy, and after a little reconnaissance, Xavier realizes she is having an affair with another soldier, much like in Macarthur's backstory, though the younger, gruffer Xavier is very unlike the original Macarthur. Xavier sabotages some training exercises, causing an unsuspecting soldier to inadvertently shoot and kill the man who impregnated Xavier's wife. Xavier receives a nasty chest wound and dies after a tense scene where Dr. Victoria Deshotel points a gun at the others, having previously tried to drown Kelly in a bathtub, thinking she was the killer. By the time Victoria attempts to patch up Xavier's wounds at the end of episode four, it is too late.

Victoria's backstory is that she tracked down the father she never knew, a highly respected surgeon, and convinced him to hire her at his clinic. A cold, arrogant man, her father first rejected her, then decided to hire her. When Victoria, who was fully sober but inexperienced, botched a surgery, killing the patient, her father flew into a rage, castigating her. He whipped himself up into such a frenzy that he gave himself a heart attack, and he died as well. Victoria is knifed in the killer's secret lair midway through episode five.

Vincent Del Piero presents himself as a lifestyle coach who promotes mental and spiritual well-being. In reality, the married man is an incorrigible womanizer who has bedded at least one underage woman. His chauffeur, who missed his dying mother's final moments in the hospital because he was transporting Vincent to his latest rendezvous, starts blackmailing him. Vincent kills his chauffeur and frames a homeless man for the crime. Vincent receives a fatal head wound, staggers around for a while, and dies at the start of the sixth and final episode.

Kelly is shown to have been involved in a criminal gang, and was tasked with seducing a rival. Her boyfriend, who gave her the dog that died on the island, was deeply in love with her and wanted her to run away with him. Instead, she turned him over to the gang members, who killed him. Kelly is later found stabbed and dumped in the pool, and when Nina sees Malik crouched over Kelly's body, she shoots him.

Malik and Nina's backstories are told over several episodes. Malik was not always devoted to charity. He once worked for a cutthroat corporation, and he dealt in all sorts of dirty tricks to get a leg up over his equally ambitious co-worker. That all changed one night when Malik was charged with a time-sensitive job, and his car broke down outside a crowded bar. Needing a vehicle, Malik stole a stranger's keys and car, but before he could reach his destination, he ran over a cyclist. Malik initially tells Nina he reported the accident, but later admits he was lying, and that he actually drove away from the scene. He returned the stolen car, and the innocent owner was arrested for the hit-and-run and died in prison.

Nina's backstory is much like Vera's. As a student, she fell in love with her married professor, and got a job as his son's nanny to be closer to her lover. As it turns out, her boyfriend's wife was aware of their affair, and warns

Nina that her husband will never leave her or his son. Nina, not believing her, convinces herself that if the boy, who suffers from diabetes, were to die, that her boyfriend would end his marriage. She allows the boy to tire himself out in the pool, leading to his drowning. Her lover did not leave his wife for her after all. Wracked with guilt, Nina hangs herself.

Mathieu and Leonie arrive at the island, and Mathieu finds Eve still alive. She faked her death with the help of Kelly, and was responsible for all the murders, inspired in part by her husband, an undercover officer disguised as a homeless man, who died of a heart attack because all the passersby thought he was a bum and refused to help him. It is not made clear how she learned about the others' crimes. There is no way Mathieu could possibly know for certain that Eve is the killer, but they silently lock eyes for a few seconds, which is apparently enough for Mathieu to see into her soul. Eve goes out into the sea, where she presumably drowns. Mathieu tries to rescue her, but cannot, and Leonie has to drag him to shore. The miniseries ends with Mathieu and Leonie sitting on the beach, looking surprisingly cheerful for being on an island with ten human corpses and a dead dog on it, and a woman drowning in the water nearby.

Notably, in this adaptation, the characters are more emotional and fearful than in prior adaptations, and much of the drama comes from frantic people suspecting each other. As radically different as *Ils étaient dix* is from the source material, the ways it borrows and reshapes from the original tale are evident to the attentive viewer.[2]

[1] *"Ils étaient dix,"* *The Internet Movie Database*, accessed July 5, 2025, *The Internet Movie Database*, accessed July 5, 2025.

[2] *Ils étaient dix*, directed by Pascal Laugier, Escazal Films/Federation Entertainment/BE-FILMS, 2020, approx.. 4 hrs. 30 min., DVD.

Chapter Thirty-Three

Other Filmed Adaptations

And Then There Were None is a global phenomenon, and there are numerous foreign-language adaptations of the book and play, mostly for television. Most of the episodes are unavailable for viewing. Some may be lost, and some may not have been recorded for posterity in the first place. Many non-English adaptations have never been subtitled or dubbed. Most of these international adaptations were episodes of anthology television series.

A ninety-minute UK production was broadcast in 1949. Perhaps the most notable aspect of this live broadcast was that one supposedly dead character got up and walked offstage, unaware he was still on camera. This gaffe supposedly upset Christie immensely.[1]

In 1956, a Polish series whose title translates to *Television Theatre* broadcast *Bylo 10 Murzynków* broadcast an adaptation.

A 1957 Brazilian adaptation was titled *O Caso dos Dez Negrinhos*, and another Brazilian adaptation came in 1963 with the same title, part of the series *Grande Teatro*.

1969 saw *Zein kleine Negerlein*, a 110-minute West German production. *Au théâtre ce soir*, a French series, aired an adaptation in 1970.

A Lebanese adaptation, *Achra Abid Zghar*, was broadcast in 1974, and the Greek series *To theatro tis Defteras* aired *Deka Mikroi Negroi* in 1978. The Spanish series *Los misterios de Laura* (the show was later Americanized into a series starring Debra Messing) often drew upon classic mystery novels, and the 2011 two-parter, whose title translates to "The Mystery of the Ten Strangers," is inspired by Christie's work).[2]

[1] Morgan, 272.

[2] "Agatha Christie," *The Internet Movie Database*, accessed July 5, 2025, https://www.imdb.com/name/nm0002005/?ref_=fn_all_nme_1.

V

PART FIVE: Miscellaneous Adaptations &
And Then There Were None's Lasting
Legacy

Chapter Thirty-Four

The Title

Many readers with a little background knowledge regarding the history of *And Then There Were None* know that the current title is not the original name of Christie's book. The original title used a much more offensive ethnic slur, which was the common title of a popular nursery rhyme in England. (Due to current objections over using it, even in a scholarly/historical context, it will not be specifically named.) The term in question was not just applied to people of African heritage in early-twentieth-century England—it was also applied to people of Asian Indian heritage, and some people applied it to other individuals of non-Caucasian backgrounds. At the time in England, the term was often used without realization of the offense or anger that might be caused. From the very start, American editions changed the title to *And Then There Were None*, with an alternate title switching the ethnicity in the rhyme. At the start of the twenty-first century, *And Then There Were None* became the official title of the book, though many European countries were slow to adopt this title.

For the purposes of easy comparison, the common British version of the rhyme, the one used in Christie's book, is repeated here:

TEN LITTLE SOLDIER BOYS

Ten Little Soldier Boys went out to dine;
One choked his little self and then there were nine.

Nine Little Soldier Boys stayed up very late;
One overslept himself and then there were eight.
Eight Little Soldier Boys travelling in Devon;
One said he'd stay there and then there were seven.
Seven Little Soldier Boys chopping up sticks;
One chopped himself in halves and then there were six.
Six Little Soldier Boys playing with a hive;
A bumblebee stung one and then there were five.
Five Little Soldier Boys going in for law;
One got in Chancery and then there were four.
Four Little Soldier Boys going out to sea;
A red herring swallowed one and then there were three.
Three Little Soldier Boys walking in the Zoo;
A big bear hugged one and then there were two.
Two Little Soldier Boys sitting in the sun;
One got frizzled up and then there was one.
One Little Soldier Boy left all alone;
He went and hanged himself and then there were none.

There was a common American version of the rhyme, and a popular version (there were many variants that used different verses) used "Indian boys," often slurred into a five-letter term which is often considered offensive. This version is attributed to Septimus Winter, and is thought to have been written in the 1860s. The rhyme reads as follows, though it often received slight variations in wording (the ethnic terms have once again been replaced with "Soldier" for the purposes of this history):

Ten little Soldiers standin' in a line,
One toddled home and then there were nine;
Nine little Soldiers swingin' on a gate,
One tumbled off and then there were eight.
Eight little Soldiers gayest under heav'n.
One went to sleep and then there were seven;
Seven little Soldiers cuttin' up their tricks,
One broke his neck and then there were six.

Six little Soldiers all alive,
One kicked the bucket and then there were five;
Five little Soldiers on a cellar door,
One tumbled in and then there were four.
Four little Soldiers up on a spree,
One got fuddled and then there were three;
Three little Soldiers out on a canoe,
One tumbled overboard and then there were two.
Two little Soldiers foolin' with a gun,
One shot t'other and then there was one;
One little Soldier livin' all alone,
He got married and then there were none.

There was a chorus that might be omitted, sometimes inserted after each couplet, occasionally sung after every fourth line:

One little, two little, three little, four little,
five little Soldier boys,
Six little, seven little, eight little, nine little,
ten little Soldier boys.

While some people viewed the rhyme as a simple counting tale, other critics argue that the narrative reflects a desensitization towards policies that led to the deaths of huge numbers of people. When the rhyme made its way to England, many of the rhymes were changed by various people, and Christie used the version with which she was most familiar. There are two clear "Britishisms" in Christie's version—the references to Devon and Chancery. Though there are American areas named after the British county of Devon, the term "Chancery" is not applied to American law courts.

In America, altering Christie's titles was a fairly common habit for much of the twentieth century. *Murder on the Orient Express*, for example, was initially titled *Murder on the Calais Coach* in the United States in order to avoid confusion with Graham Greene's contemporaneous novel *Murder on the Orient Express*. United States publishers tried to "Americanize" titles they thought were "too British." *Lord Edgware Dies*, featuring the name of a peer of the realm, was altered to *Thirteen at Dinner*. Also, many American publishers were not fond of nursery rhyme titles, so they altered *Five Little Pigs* to *Murder in Retrospect*, and *Hickory Dickory Dock* was adjusted to *Hickory Dickory Death*, to name just two examples. Sometimes the changes did not make a ton of sense, such as when *The Sittaford Mystery* was changed to *The Murder at Hazelmoor*. Most of the time, publishers simply adopted a title that they thought would appeal to their prospective audience. By the mid-1990s, Christie's American publishers began pivoting back to using the original Christie titles. This may have confused many longtime readers, who suddenly discovered there were dozens of "new" books by one of their favorite authors, only to discover soon after buying the novel that they had already read it. The one novel to keep a changed title was *And Then There Were None*, for obvious reasons. Some readers think this title gives away the ending, while others appreciate it for its dark and forbidding tone. Agatha Christie Ltd. made *And Then There Were None* the book and the play's official English title around the turn of the century.

Until the early twenty-first century, the term "Indian" was used for the rhyme and statuettes, but they were eventually replaced with the ethnically neutral word "Soldiers." Other passages using comparable terminology have been edited or deleted in recent editions.

And Then There Were None has been criticized for including passages where certain characters speak negatively of Black or Jewish people, but this is actually important characterization, as the unsettling and bigoted sides of certain characters are developed to show the odious aspects of their personalities. Even though Christie portrayed the bigotry as a negative character quality, some late-twentieth-century editions deleted derogatory quips about Jewish people, although the current edition replaces them as a means of showing Lombard's sinister side.

Chapter Thirty-Five

The Board Game

nd Then There Were None's story went beyond the page to the stage, the screen, and also the tabletop. In 1968, the board game company Ideal released a game inspired by Christie's novel. It was one of Ideal's "Famous Mystery Classic Series," which also features the games *Murder on the Orient Express* (with Sherlock Holmes and Doctor Watson replacing Hercule Poirot!), The Case of the Elusive Assassin (featuring Ellery Queen) and Fu Manchu's Hidden Hoard. *And Then There Were None* is thought to be the hardest to find game of this quartet.

The cover of the box featured an image of a black-covered copy of *And Then There Were None* on the left, with *Ten Little Indians* in tiny letters in parentheses underneath the title. The cover featured a white-haired man in a grey three-piece suit rising out of a chair with his arms outstretched, as a man in a long dark coat is seen from behind firing a gun at him. While the scene might reference Wargrave's death in the book, readers will know full well that this is not how the Judge actually died. On a table in front of the shooter are several statuettes of Native Americans, a couple of which are toppled over.

The information sheets and another part of the box featured an image of two similar-looking men in suits kneeling on the ground next to the body of a man in a suit, lying several inches away from a large rock. The living man on the right is holding a revolver, making that image a parallel to Lombard, though the scene does not precisely portray any scene in the book, as Doctor Armstrong discovered the General's body on his own, and it was Vera who was with Lombard when Blore and Armstrong's bodies were found.

The blue plastic tray holding the game's supplies featured two heads of Native Americans wearing traditional headdresses facing each other. Off to the left was a pack of cards for playing the game, and in the center were four playing pieces shaped like human figures with undefinable features. One token was red, another green, one white, and one blue. The white figure appears to be holding a magnifying glass. The information sheets were stored in the lower right of the tray, and a die was kept below the playing pieces.

The game board was divided into thirteen sections, representing the house and grounds of Judge Wargrave's residence. The "start" section represented the front steps of the house, and was located at the six o'clock position on the board. Going clockwise, the remaining outdoor sections of the board were the west lawn (covering the lower left portion of the board), the patio (covering a stripe of the left side), the rear lawn (the top of the board), the beach (encompassing a stripe on the right side of the board, and the east lawn on the lower right part of the board. The words *"And Then There Were None* by Agatha Christie" are written on the sand of the beach.

The rooms of the house are not marked, but they are identifiable by the furniture and other items. The two rooms on the left side of the house appear to be the billiard room and the library, with the billiard room on top. A corridor divides the center of the house, and the top right corner has a small bedroom to the left and a kitchen to the right. Right below is a dining room, with a lounge in the lower right corner of the house. Doors are strategically placed around the house to limit the ways in which players can move.

The rooms of *And Then There Were None's* board are markedly more gruesome than the ones on the board for *Clue*, with nine bodies scattered throughout the house and grounds. The following names reflect how the characters are identified in the game. General Macarthur is sprawled out on the ground of the patio, while Dr. Armstrong is floating in the water right next to the shore of the beach. Vera Claythorne lies in the chair behind the desk in the library with a rope around her neck. The top half of Capt. Lombard's body is sprawled out on the billiard table while his lifeless legs prop him up upon the floor, and Mr. Blore's body lies on its back in the center of the corridor. Mrs. Rodgers is face down on the bed in her room, and Mr. Rodgers lies on his back on the kitchen tiles. Anthony Marston sits at the head of the dining room table and has fallen forward upon the table with his arms outstretched. Finally, a brown-haired Emily Brent wearing a dress with a hemline that is rather shorter than anything the character in the book would have worn is lying face down on the lounge's blue carpet with her arms in the ten-minutes-past-seven position.

At the start of the game, all the players are dealt cards. The person with the #1 card (featuring Wargrave's picture) is the killer. Over the course of the game, the players move between the rooms and outside areas, asking the other players questions about their cards. The killer can either lie or tell the truth, while the other players must respond truthfully. If one of the innocent players can identify the killer and what cards that player holds, that person wins the game. If the "murderer" can figure out what cards the others are holding before getting caught, that player wins.[1]

* * *

More recently, a Spanish-language game titled *10 Negritos* was released in 2014 by Peka Editorial. In this game, with an ominous-looking island getting struck by lightning on the box, there are multiple playing settings and levels. Players have to work together in teams, as characters are slain, and the players have to form teams with the characters and perform various quests. After dealing numerous different kinds of cards, the players must utilize each character's unique abilities and uncover hidden secrets, identifying the killer while players are eliminated from play one by one. The goal is to identify both the killer and the killer's accomplice before time expires and all the characters are dead. In another form of game play, one of the players is the murderer, unbeknownst to the others.

In 2015, there were plans to release an English-language version, possibly in conjunction with the release of the BBC miniseries, but this never came to fruition. As of this writing, attempts to produce an English-language edition have not yet succeeded.[2]

[1] "And Then There Were None (Ten Little Indians) (1968)," *Board Game Geek*, https://boardgamegeek.com/boardgame/11387/and-then-there-were-none-ten-little-indians.

[2] "Diez Negritos (board game)," Agatha Christie Wiki, accessed July 6, 2025, https://agathachristie.fandom.com/wiki/Diez_Negritos_(board_game).

Chapter Thirty-Six

The First Graphic Novel Adaptation

From the mid-1990s to the early 2010s, many of Agatha Christie's mysteries were adapted into graphic novels by a variety of authors. *And Then There Were None* was one of the first. In 1996, Francois Rivière, a French writer, condensed the story into forty-six pages, and the tale was illustrated by Frank Leclercq, a Belgian artist.

The graphic novel followed the book closely. It opens in 1938, and the events of the book are told in essentially the same order as in the original story, with no significant changes to the characterizations. Dialogue is reduced to a minimum, and many panels are wordless, yet the story and all of the important details are included. Isaac Morris and his murder are absent. The statuettes are soldier boys, resembling British beefeaters.

The depictions of the characters are completely original and bear no resemblance to any of the major actors who have played the roles in the past. Vera wears clothes that look rather more fashionable than someone on a games mistress's salary could afford, and her hair is short and dark. In the flashback scenes, Vera has substantially longer hair. Whenever the characters reflect on their past misdeeds, the panels are tinted red. The same coloring effect is used in the scene where the characters are accused by the record.

Lombard has a little moustache, a detail that was briefly mentioned in the original novel, and none of the major actors who play the role on-screen in English-language adaptations have sported facial hair. Lombard's hair is blondish red, and he rather resembles Colonel Mustard as he was drawn in some of the earliest British versions of the board game Cluedo (Clue for American players). The comparison is aided by the fact that he often wears a mustard-yellow shirt. Blore is stockily built, with black hair, and a vague resemblance to Edward G. Robinson. Dr. Armstrong appears to be one of the younger characters, with wavy brown hair, and wears a green suit and tie for most of the story.

Justice Wargrave is drawn as a dignified figure with white hair, usually in a blue-green suit, and at times his face is warm, even kindly. Less sympathetic-looking is Emily Brent, whose face is wrinkled and her expression is perpetually bitter. She has short white hair, her skin is darker than that of most of the other characters, and her eyes are obscured by dark glasses, which only occasionally become translucent. Rogers is portrayed as having salt-and-pepper hair, and his face is nondescript. General Macarthur is given dramatic white hair and a prominent moustache, rather like Colonel Mustard as drawn by Drew Struzan in the 1990s. Mrs. Rogers appears rather younger than she is often portrayed on film, with a bun of honey-colored hair and a worried, bitter expression. Anthony Marston has curly dark hair and a smug look on his face most of the time.

This is one of the few adaptations to include the conversation between the two Scotland Yard detectives as they discuss the murders and the seeming impossibility of the crime. Before the truth of the crime is revealed, there is a full page, colored like a brown wooden board, with pictures of the ten suspects in a five-by-two grid, with a red question mark superimposed over them, along with a statement about the discovery made years later by a fishing trawler.

A disproportionate amount of the graphic novel is devoted to the last thirty pages of the book, with multiple pages showing Vera's last moments, and the killer's suicide is shown step by step. Though many of the corpses are shown, as are some of the actual murders being committed, the gore is minimal, aside from one of the last panels, where the killer's suicide wound is shown clearly.

Overall, this is a concise retelling of *And Then There Were None*, focusing on the heart of the story and effectively using artwork to advance the narrative and develop characterization.[1]

[1] Agatha Christie, François Riviére, and Frank Leclercq, *And Then There Were None* (HarperCollins, 2009), 1-48.

Chapter Thirty-Seven

Ils étaient dix Graphic Novel (2020)

A second graphic novel adaptation, the French-language *Ils étaient dix*, was released by Paquet in 2020. As of this writing, it has not been translated into English. It covers the overwhelming majority of the original novel, though it places more emphasis on text than the previous adaptation, which had large portions devoted solely to images. Pascal Davoz adapted the novel, the artwork was drawn by Callixte, and Georges Van Linthout provided the coloring.

In this graphic novel, the ten little soldiers are all identical red-jacketed beefeaters. Wargrave is drawn as a lean, gray-haired man with a slightly receded hairline and a small moustache, plus round glasses. Vera is an attractive young blonde, whereas Lombard is in early middle-age, his brown hair flecked with gray at the temples. He also sports a goatee. Emily Brent has short hair and wears round sunglasses, so her eyes are rarely visible. The General is a strongly built man with short gray hair and a moustache. Doctor Armstrong has light brown hair and is clean-shaven. Marston has black wavy hair and a perpetual five o'clock shadow. Blore is a stocky man with pale hair and a snub nose. Rogers is a thin man with light brown hair, and Mrs. Rogers is blonde, appearing much younger and prettier than she is commonly depicted. Hugo is shown briefly in flashback as a young, dark-haired man with a pencil moustache. Morris's short flashback scene shows him sporting black hair with a widow's peak and glasses.

When the characters are accused by the record, the panels are divided into a three-by-three grid, with each character accused in turn. Notably, Mrs. Rogers is not included in the panel accusing her, only her husband. Marston's death does not occur until nearly halfway through the graphic novel, and the deaths occur in rapid succession afterwards.

One of the major alterations to the original story is that the bottle with Wargrave's confession is no longer retrieved by the *Emma Jane* fishing trawler, but instead was found by a British soldier being evacuated at Dunkirk in 1940. In a bit of irony, it is shown that the Scotland Yard detectives passed within feet of the floating bottle as they were ferried to (or possibly from) the island, but they did not notice it. In the final panels, the Scotland Yard detectives are shown looking over the manuscript and reacting to the revelations.

There are a few grisly scenes. When Arthur Richmond is killed on the battlefield by a German sniper, a small fountain of blood spurts from his forehead. There is a bloody drawing of Blore's head crushed by the bear clock, and blood is shown spurting from the back of the General's head when Wargrave strikes him. In this graphic novel, the weapon used to kill the General is a shovel. In some flashback scenes, Armstrong's hands are covered in blood at the time of the fatal surgery. The doctor's hand is again stained when he touches the "wound" on Wargrave's forehead. A single shot is not enough to kill Lombard at the end—Vera fires five times. Vera is also shown twisting in the noose during her death scene.

Vera's character often wears revealing clothing. Additionally, midway through the adaptation, when Vera remembers her time with Hugo, she is shown wearing only her underwear, painting her toenails. A couple of Vera's outfits display cleavage.

Some of the clothing choices are a bit more casual at times than they are often portrayed as being in adaptations. In his final scene on the beach with Vera, Lombard is dressed a lot like Indiana Jones.

Overall, this is a stylish, efficient adaptation that is largely loyal to the source material.

Chapter Thirty-Eight

Radio/Audio Adaptations

Over the decades, most of Christie's novels have been adapted for radio, and in most of the BBC productions, the results have been remarkably faithful to the books, far more so than in the lion's share of the film and television adaptations. On December 27, 1947, Ayton Whitaker dramatized the book for the BBC Home Service's Monday Matinee, under the original title. It was rerun for the BBC Light Programme's *Saturday Night Theatre* two days later.[1] It is not readily available to listeners, and may be lost, like many productions from that era.

Sixty-three years later, a BBC Radio 4 *Saturday Play* adaptation of *And Then There Were None*, with Mary Peate as the director and Joy Wilkinson as the author, was broadcast on November 13, 2010.

The 2010 radio adaptation hews pretty closely to the original novel, keeping much of the original dialogue and following the book's plot almost scene for scene, though certain scenes are naturally compressed and abridged to fit the eighty-five-minute runtime. The first murder does not occur until a third of the way through the play, and by the end, the deaths occur at a fairly swift and steady clip.

The cast of the radio adaptation is as follows.

Lyndsey Marahal: Vera Claythorne
Alex Wyndham: Captain Lombard
Sam Dale: Mr. Blore

Sean Baker: Dr. Armstrong
Geoffrey Whitehead: Mr. Justice Wargrave
Joanna Monro: Emily Brent
Wayne Foskett: Mr. Rogers
John Rowe: General Macarthur
Sally Orrock: Mrs. Rogers
Lloyd Thomas: Anthony Marston
Harry Child: Cyril
Adeel Akhtar: Narrator
Henry Devas: Hugo
Jude Akuwudike: Gramophone Voice[2]

There are a few changes. Cyril is introduced in the opening flashback scene, and his character voices each couplet of the poem as each character is killed. Miss Brent kills the bee that has been released into the room right before she dies, and Blore is killed with a rock, not a bear clock. Furthermore, Rogers' death is made even more grisly, as he has been "hacked to pieces." The biggest alteration is in the climactic scene, where Wargrave confronts Vera and tells her everything. When she tries to turn the revolver on him, he informs her that he only left one bullet in the gun when he returned it, so after it was used on Lombard, it is empty. In this version, though Seton was guilty, Wargrave admits to crossing a line with excessively vindictive summing-up, but says he broke the law for a righteous purpose. When Wargrave informs Vera that Hugo told him what really happened to Cyril and then hung himself, Vera completely breaks down and commits suicide by hanging in front of him. After taking a few moments to tidy up, Wargrave shoots himself without making it clear he will make his death look like murder. As is usual, the penultimate scene with the Scotland Yard detectives is completely absent, and Isaac Morris has also been cut.[3]

Overall, the 2010 BBC radio production is one of the most faithful adaptations of the original novel yet created.

In September 2024, an audio adaptation of *And Then There Were None* was created in Bengali. It was broadcast on the radio station Mirchi Bangla as an entry in their regular program, "Sunday Suspense." The show was also released on the app Gaana. The promotional materials featured a picture of a gun with six bullets next to it. The gun was covered in streaks of blood.[4]

[1] "Ten Little Ni**ers (BBC Home Service Adaptation)," Agatha Christie Wiki, accessed July 6, 2025, https://agathachristie.fandom.com/wiki/Ten_Little_Ni**ers_(BBC_Home_Service_adaptation).

[2] "And Then There Were None (BBC Radio 4 Adaptation)," Agatha Christie Wiki, accessed July 6 2025, https://agathachristie.fandom.com/wiki/And_Then_There_Were_None_(BBC_Radio_4_adaptation).

[3] Agatha Christie and Joy Wilkinson, *And Then There Were None: A BBC Radio 4 Full Cast Dramatization*, BBC, released 2011, CD.

[4] "Sunday Suspense | And Then There Were None | Agatha Christie | Mirchi Bangla," *YouTube*, uploaded by Mirchi Bagla, September 29, 2024, https://www.youtube.com/watch?v=bVHetS2IFWs.

Chapter Thirty-Nine

The Computer Game

And Then There Were None has successfully been adapted for the stage and screen. Could it work as an interactive computer game? In 2005, The Adventure Company revealed their answer to this question.

In this point-and-click game, the players can take on the role of Patrick Narracott, the brother of Fred Narracott, the ferryman in the original book. He is not an entirely original character, as in the novel, there is a fleeting reference to Narracott having a brother who covers for his sibling when he is ill. This brother is not named in the book, though. Patrick takes the guests to the island, which is the only contemporary adaptation to change the rhyme to "Ten Little Sailors" and to rechristen the setting "Shipwreck Island" (viewed from a distance, a rock alongside the isle looks like a sinking ship, and during storms, it is easy for an unwary sailor to crash a boat into a hidden rock in the sea.). Patrick has taken over for Fred because his brother has been wrongly accused of being a thief, and Patrick seeks to clear his sibling's name. Though mentioned occasionally, Fred only appears at the very end, in one of the game's four possible endings.

As it turns out, Blore is responsible for falsely accusing Fred, and Blore scuttles Patrick's dinghy, mistaking him for his brother and seeking a confrontation to capture a believed criminal. Trapped on the island, Patrick is compelled to investigate as his fellow guests are murdered one by one. No matter what happens, Patrick survives, but the player's actions in the closing scenes of the game determine whether Vera, Lombard, or both also emerge unscathed.

Most of the game follows the book's plot reasonably closely. As Patrick, the player spends much of the game exploring the house and the grounds of the island. The number of locations has been expanded substantially from the book. In addition to the bedrooms and other main rooms of the house, there is a secret underground cavern complete with tunnels, and there are many fields, outbuildings, and historical artifacts around the island. Gameplay is divided into ten "chapters," each beginning with the corresponding couplet from the poem, and culminating in a homicide.

Progression in the game requires a combination of interviewing suspects, solving puzzles, and completing tasks. Puzzles include rearranging lettered drawers to spell out a secret message, and finding items around the island and combining them to form new items that can be used to move the story forward. Some notable tasks involve using a bushel of fresh apples and a bushel of fermented apples to make juice and cider, and then using the beverages to persuade a suspect to talk, or to make the brambles blocking a path more palatable to a hungry goat, thereby allowing Patrick to walk to a new destination after the goat has eaten up the brambles. In another instance, Patrick must gather up sheets, a harness, and other various items from around the island to create a glider in the hopes of flying to the mainland (it does not work),

As for the plot, it remains largely the same aside from the fact that most of the storylines center around Patrick's adventures. Most of the cut scenes are based on passages from the book. Some of the alterations are small, while others are much more significant. Many of the deaths are mildly changed. The weapon used to bludgeon General MacArthur to death is never specified for certain in the book, but in the game, the use of a large rock from the beach is suspected shortly after the discovery of the body and confirmed in an epilogue. Rogers dies of a blow to the head from an axe in the book, but in the game he is literally chopped in half at the waist, and the segments of his corpse are spread apart, though the gory wounds are discreetly hidden by a large woodpile, and only the parts of Rogers from the middle of his back up and his thighs down are visible. The game never makes it clear whether or not Rogers was killed or otherwise incapacitated before his body was so horribly severed, nor is it explained how the killer's clothing was protected from huge amounts of gore and blood spatter. Emily Brent is not slain with a syringe full of poison, as she is in the book. In the game, her potentially fatal allergy to bee stings is referenced early in the game, and she is found covered in welts by the island's apiary. While in the game, Wargrave fakes his own death by gunshot wound as he does in the book, he meets his ultimate fate in the game by a blow to the head from a massive law book he wrote himself. Throughout the game, there is a subplot about a growing love triangle between Patrick, Vera, and Lombard. The attraction of both men to Vera is obvious early on, and at one point Lombard and Vera cozy up together on the couch in the screening room, watching a film.

Finally, the fates of Lombard and Vera depend on a pair of choices the player makes late in the game. In the two endings where Lombard dies, he is not shot, as in the book, but instead is killed in an explosion caused by a bomb in the bonfire he built on a cliff in order to signal to the mainland for help. If Narracott rushes to the bonfire immediately after speaking to a frightened Vera late in the novel, he gets there in time to warn Lombard away from the explosion, and Lombard reveals that he is actually Charles

Morley, a twist taken from the 1945 screenplay rather than Christie's novel or her own stage adaptation. The real Lombard committed suicide, and Morley took his place to investigate. If Narracott dawdles and visits other locations first, when he finally arrives at the bonfire site, Lombard is already dead. In the pair of endings where Vera perishes, the killer holds her at gunpoint and provides a lengthy explanation of the crimes. If Narracott throws a piece of the marble bear clock (retrieved from where Blore's body was found) at the killer's hand, he knocks away the revolver and saves Vera's life. If Narracott does anything else, Vera is shot and killed. No matter what happens, Narracott wrestles with U.N. Owen, and a final push sends the killer over the landing and into a noose originally meant for Vera dangling from the ceiling, thereby hanging the culprit.

In the first possible closing scene, the brothers Narracott flee for Australia, as they have no proof that Fred is innocent, and Patrick knows that the police will arrest the sole survivor of the carnage on Shipwreck Island. If only Morley/Lombard survives, he promises to let the authorities know Fred is innocent, having heard Blore's confession, and the two men part as friends. If just Vera lives, she reveals that her boyfriend Hugo convinced Cyril to swim to the rock and drown, and that she is innocent. Additionally, her testimony about Blore's confession will clear Fred. Patrick observes that there's an alternative ending to the rhyme about getting married, and the pair kiss. The fourth ending, where both Morley/Lombard and Vera escape, is an amalgam of the previous endings where only one survives, using the same animations and dialogue blended together. In this ending, Morley/Lombard rides away with a smile, showing no jealousy over Vera and Patrick being together.

The biggest change from the books is the identity of U.N. Owen. In order to provide a surprise for players, Emily Brent is the killer– and she is actually an imposter who has assumed Brent's identity. The murderer is actually a once-famous actress named Gabrielle Steele (a reference to the Hollywood actress Gabrielle Turl, who is fleetingly mentioned as being a rumored purchaser of the island in the book's opening scenes). Steele's films are referenced occasionally over the course of the game, and some posters of her movies hang in the screening room.

In the denouement, Patrick watches from a distance as Brent/Steele points the revolver at Vera and confesses. Steele had a nervous breakdown acting in the film *The Last of the Borgias*, which may have been the start of her homicidal madness. She played Lillian Borgia and claims that her character entered her psyche, leading her to attack her co-star. Though he survived, the scandal wrecked her career. Steele was in love with Edward Seton, and when Wargrave bullied Seton over the course of three days of a brutal trial, Seton killed himself (as opposed to being hanged by the authorities). Steele vowed to get revenge by killing Wargrave and planned for him to suffer for three days of mental strain, just as Seton had. She devised the plan for not only murdering him, but also others who killed and could not be prosecuted.

Steele killed the real Brent and assumed her identity. Nearly halfway through committing the murders, she faked her own death by smearing her face with the irritant Bellman's Universal Embrocation so the resulting irritated blemishes resembled bee stings and lying still. Consuming a little curare helped disguise her pulse. This curare was tucked into a ring with a receptacle for holding poison, a souvenir from the movie, which was previously used to kill Marston and Mrs. Rogers (it must have been able to hold two separate poisons). She had previously riled up Dr. Armstrong by taunting him over his crime, causing him to consume so much alcohol that he was unable to properly examine her and determine that she was still alive.

She was stunned to find that someone had murdered Wargrave before she had, but as soon as she discovered that Wargrave was alive and performing his own investigation, she bludgeoned him with his own law book.

Isaac Morris becomes Archibald Morris, a lawyer who helped Steele perform the research to find eight more people (aside from the already-targeted Brent and Wargrave) who got away with murder. Eager to accept the copious amounts of money Steele offered him, Morris did not ask questions. Steele killed Morris in an unspecified manner to keep him quiet. As Morris's quasi-legal activities led to miscarriages of justice, Steele believed killing him was justified.

There are several clues to the new solution that have been sprinkled throughout the game, including a large makeup kit in Brent's room, which draws attention because she is not the kind of woman who should be interested in cosmetics. The makeup is used to make Steele look older, plainer, and at one point, deader. The words "Three Days" are scratched on the wall of the screening room, a reference to the amount of time that Seton suffered in Wargrave's courtroom, and the duration for which Steele wished Wargrave to agonize as well. At one point in the game, Brent/Steele angrily refers to "three days" to Wargrave, foreshadowing her plan. The location of the bottle of Bellman's Universal Embrocation, close to the apiary where Brent/Steele was found, is another clue, as the canny player, knowing that the substance causes a rash, will be suspicious. These suspicions will be confirmed if the player thinks to dust the embrocation bottle for fingerprints (several items can be fingerprinted throughout the game for clues) and finds only Emily Brent's prints on it.

In all four endings, Brent/Steele meets her end exactly the same way. She attacks Patrick, and the two wrestle for a few seconds before Patrick shoves her over the landing railing in self-defense. By an incredible coincidence, Brent/Steele's head falls right into the noose (What are the odds? Surely it would be quite difficult to achieve such a feat, even if one aimed the head of the person being thrown at the noose), and as her body falls, she is hanged. It is an ironic ending, as the rhyme is fulfilled by sheer chance. Incidentally, the actual hanging is not fully shown on-screen. Only Brent/Steele's feet and the lower part of her legs are pictured, dangling in the air.

As is often the case with changes to Christie's plots, some of the alterations are often illogical under close scrutiny. Other alterations add mysterious twists to the game, and others add comedy, albeit somewhat accidentally.

One twist is added to Anthony Marston's character. As the first to die, his role is usually one of the briefest in the narrative, along with Mrs. Rogers. In the game, Patrick runs into Anthony soon after he discovers his boat has been scuttled. A brief conversation makes it seem as if Anthony was up to something shady. Over the course of the game, a coded message and a rumor passed on by another guest indicate that Marston may have been a spy for the Nazis, who have been considering capturing the island and using it as a naval base in a planned invasion of England, tying into the 1939 pre-WWII setting. It is an intriguing plot point, but it is not developed further and plays no significant role in the mystery or the solution.

Another side quest that ultimately makes little sense takes place shortly after Miss Brent's "murder." While the surviving guests eat, Patrick suddenly feels unwell and discovers that the word "Solidamide" has been written beneath his plate. Dr. Armstrong explains that Solidamide is a deadly poison, but its effects can be reversed through the consumption of turpentine oil, found in substances like Bellman's Universal Embrocation, which can cause nasty skin eruptions in large doses. (Solidamide, incidentally, is a purely fictional substance created for the game.) Patrick must then launch a search for a bottle of Bellman's Universal Embrocation. Given the number of locations and potential hiding places, this can be a frustrating and time-consuming chore, and when one finally finds the location of the bottle of embrocation, just past the apiary, it consists of just a couple of small golden pixels, easy for the player to miss, especially if one's eyes are weary from staring for a long time at the screen. If the player takes a while to find the antidote, Patrick will occasionally comment on how poorly he's feeling. In any case, Patrick gulps down the embrocation and is instantly in excellent health for a man who was just minutes away from death moments earlier.

The critical thinker will no doubt wonder, did U.N. Owen really plan to kill Patrick? After all, with no reference to law or Chancery, and a murder that fit those criteria planned for another character, Patrick's death by poison would not fit the rhyme at that point. Not only that, but Patrick was not a murderer, which means that there is no abstract justice justification for killing him. Furthermore, if U.N. Owen really wanted to kill Patrick, why write the name of the poison on the back of the plate, or use something with a ready antidote? It seems that U.N. Owen wanted to give Patrick a chance to survive. But if so, why leave the bottle of Bellman's Universal Embrocation where it was? Patrick might have put two and two together, as the savvy player will, to realize the significance of finding the bottle there. Surely it would have been wiser to hide the bottle elsewhere, even if the goal was to send Patrick away for whatever reason. Ultimately, the solidamide side quest is one of the more tedious and time-consuming problems to solve, and in the context of the game, it seems like a highly illogical action on the part of the killer.

One aspect of the game that is rather darkly humorous when one thinks about it is the fact that Patrick is expected to sleep downstairs on the couch in the parlor, as there is no bedroom available for him when he reveals he has to stay the night. This is reasonable at first, but then Marston dies, and his body is placed in his bed. It is rather hard luck on Patrick, as a dead man is given a more comfortable and private place to rest than he is. Of course, it is easier for Patrick to snoop around downstairs on his own downstairs that first night, but considering the fact that more beds are freed up over the next couple of days, and that a locked room is safer for a guest that the open parlor, it seems most unfair to Patrick that the dead are treated with more consideration than he is. Even more unsettling is the fact that Thomas and Ethel Rogers sleep in twin beds. In the novel and some adaptations, the butler moves into a spare room or the woodshed after his wife dies, but in this game, the player can wonder just how well Rogers slept three feet away from his wife's corpse!

Furthermore, even though every character except Narracott has brought plenty of luggage, everybody wears the same outfit day after day until they either die or are rescued.

After whichever of the four endings plays, there is one final twist. The game cuts back to Patrick in an empty house, where he must take the last little sailor boy and place it in a little indentation shaped like the figurine's feet (the observant viewer will have caught this detail earlier in the game). Placing the sailor boy in the indentation will lead to a panel opening, revealing a reel of film. Playing the film in the projector reveals the original ending, consisting of Wargrave's written confession, which was indeed placed in a bottle, thrown into the sea, and retrieved. The events of the narrative are retold with Wargrave as the killer, and the dialogue is very similar to the last chapter of the book, with a few additions, such as Wargrave's justification for his suicide. This video consists of the written confession scrolling up the screen, with images and video of the characters, settings, and other pertinent images superimposed upon the text. In the scene showing the General's death, a silhouette of Wargrave is shown holding a large rock over his head, illustrating the weapon that was never identified in the books.[2]

The game produced wide-ranging critical responses, with the puzzles, character design, and adaptation all provoking varying assessments depending on the evaluator. In the initial PC release of the game, a paperback copy of *And Then There Were None* was included alongside the CD-ROMs. Despite the mixed reactions, the game was sufficiently successful to be adapted for the Wii console, and numerous other computer game adaptations of Christie novels were released over the coming decade. Two more interactive games based on *Murder on the Orient Express* and *Evil Under the Sun* followed in 2006 and 2007, respectively. Two very different video game adaptations of *The ABC Murders* were released in 2009 and 2016, and four hidden object games based on *Death on the Nile, Peril at End House, Dead Man's Folly*, and *4:50 from Paddington* were made available between 2007 and 2010, as well as a game very loosely inspired by the Harley Quin stories. The computer game adaptation of *Evil Under the Sun* features a quick reference to *And Then There Were None* in the early stages of the game. A file regarding the case labelled "Shipwreck" is in Poirot's office, implying that he has either been looking into the mystery (indicating that the unhappiest of the game's four endings occurred), or he is simply studying a notable solved case out of professional interest (meaning that any of the game's three other endings happened). The file contains a newspaper cutting with the headline "Nightmare on Shipwreck Island," with no specific number of deaths mentioned.[3] Other video game adaptations of *Murder on the Orient Express* (in a modernized setting) and *Death on the Nile* have been released, as well games based on Poirot's younger years, plus a few others.

[1] "Agatha Christie: And Then There Were None (Video Game, 2005)," The Internet Movie Database, accessed July 6, 2025, https://www.imdb.com/titl e/tt0478091/?ref_=nm_flmg_job_1_cdt_t_66.

[2] Awe Productions, *Agatha Christie: And Then There Were None*, The Learning Company, CD-ROM, 2005.

[3] Awe Productions, *Agatha Christie: Evil Under the Sun*, The Learning Company, CD-ROM, 2007.

Chapter Forty

The Parodies

One can tell when something's made it into the mainstream public consciousness once it starts to be parodied. A joke about a creative work will not land if very few people are familiar with it. While many serious mysteries have been inspired by *And Then There Were None*, the story has also been parodied many times, almost always affectionately. Some popular movie spoofs, like Neil Simon's *Murder by Death* and *Clue: The Movie*, use the trope of a group of people travelling to an isolated area and murders follow, but they do not incorporate more than oblique references to *And Then There Were None* into their plots. The following examples parody Christie's novel more directly. This is not a complete list of parodies, but these are some of the most famous and successful ones.

* * *

Fred Carmichael (Any Number Can Die, Done to Death)

Fred Carmichael was an actor and playwright who specialized in comedies, usually with crime-centric plots. He led the Caravan Theatre at Vermont's Dorset Playhouse during the third quarter of the twentieth century, and wrote dozens of plays, many of which were published by Samuel French. Two of his most popular plays were direct spoofs of *And Then There Were*

None. Any Number Can Die (1965) has a motley collection of characters travelling to a house on an island off the coast of North Carolina, and multiple murders follow, though there are several survivors by the end.[1] *And Then There Were None's* plot points of the killer faking his death, and a character using an alias, are included. *Done to Death* (1970) features five formerly successful mystery writers (a married couple who write sophisticated whodunits in the vein of Nick and Nora Charles, an Agatha Christie-style grande dame, a young creator of spy thrillers, and a horror writer turned hardboiled private eye novelist), are hired to collaborate to write what will hopefully become a hit television show. They are sent to the Caribbean island retreat of Vulture's Vault to brainstorm, but soon their producer is murdered, followed by more deaths. The ending mirrors the novel version of *And Then There Were None*, along with a penultimate revelation that is quite close to the ending of *Something's Afoot*, though *Done to Death* includes a couple more twists that end the show with a more upbeat tone, followed by a shocking twist. The play is filled with references to Christie and other mysteries, and the authors often mourn how their once innovative approaches to crime writing have become clichés.[2]

* * *

Something's Afoot

This 1972 musical is a clear spoof of *And Then There Were None*, as well as other classics of the genre. Written by James McDonald, David Vos, Robert Gerlach, and Ed Linderman and featuring a ten-actor cast, the plot revolves around six guests being invited to the isolated English estate of Lord Rancour in 1935. The guests consist of Miss Tweed, a spirited mystery fan reminiscent of Christie's self-parody, Mrs. Ariadne Oliver, as well as Margaret Rutherford's take on Miss Marple; the dewy-eyed ingenue Hope Landon, the serious medical man Doctor Grayburn, the aristocratic Lady Manley-Prowe, the blustering Colonel Gillweather, and Lord Rancour's ne'er-do-well, grasping nephew Nigel Rancour. They are met by the three servants, the proper butler Clive, the maid Lettie, and the handyman/gardener Flint. Later in the show, the college athlete Geoffrey arrives unexpectedly, and soon develops a reciprocal attraction to Hope.

The pleasant weekend is interrupted when Clive announces that Lord Rancour (who never appears onstage) has been shot dead. Moments later, Clive is killed by a bomb on the stairwell, and over the course of the show, characters are killed by a series of booby-traps in the mansion, including a telephone that emits poison gas, a light switch set to electrocute the user, a shrunken head hidden in the furniture that shoots toxic darts, deadly decorations, tainted decanters, and a Chinese vase with a woodchipper inside. As each character falls victim, Miss Tweed leads the investigation, culminating in the eleventh-hour number "I Owe It All," where Miss Tweed declares that her sleuthing skills come from reading lots of mystery novels, especially Agatha Christie's.

There is a strong level of suspended disbelief in the musical, as it goes beyond credulity that every victim will just happen to be standing in precisely the right place to get murdered at the right time, and indeed, three of the deaths do not fit the killer's carefully laid plans. The ending of *Something's Afoot* is actually closer to the ending of Christie's original novel than her stage adaptation, but it is played for black comedy, and given the likability of the later victims, the laughs of the dark ending are fairly blunted. Most of the victims did nothing to justify being killed.

The musical insists that in the programs, the song list should not include the traditional mention of the characters who sing each number, as such information will serve as spoilers for who dies when.[3]

Something's Afoot ran for sixty-one performances on Broadway in 1976, and a filmed stage version starring Jean Stapleton as Miss Tweed aired on television in 1982.[4] It continues to be performed regularly by local theaters, schools, and community groups.

* * *

Mathnet: The Case of the Mystery Weekend
From 1987 to 1992, American public television (PBS) taught children

mathematics on the show *Square One TV*. This half-hour series aired weekday afternoons. The first part of each episode (usually lasting fifteen to twenty minutes, though it could be a bit shorter sometimes) consisted of a repertory cast performing skits such as parodies of television shows and movies, songs, short informational presentations, magic tricks, and game shows where children would compete for prizes like sweaters and calculators.

The second part of the show was a crime serial called *Mathnet*, an affectionate parody of *Dragnet*. A pair of detectives solved various unusual crimes connected to mathematics, usually parodying classic popular culture along the way. Each storyline would be divided into five parts, one airing each weekday over the course of a week. Joe Howard played George Frankly in thirty-five-part storylines over five seasons, and was partnered with a riff on Dragnet's Joe Friday: Kate Monday (Beverly Leech) in the first three seasons, and with Pat Tuesday (Toni DiBuono) in the last two seasons. George Frankly was amiable and good-humored, and his seeming cluelessness disguised a sharp mind. Kate Monday and Pat Tuesday were both no-nonsense types who still had a taste for fun. George was happily married to the never-seen Martha, and his close friendships with his detecting partners were always strictly platonic. Midway through the series' run, the detectives were transferred from Los Angeles to New York City. In many episodes, a child or teenager would come to them for help with a problem, ranging from needing help finding a missing autographed baseball, recovering a stolen car, or clearing the name of a parent charged with bank robbery.[5]

In the fifth and final season (1992), "The Case of the Mystery Weekend," George and Pat attended a murder mystery weekend (Martha was unable to attend, so George invited Pat instead) at an isolated estate in a mountainous rural region of New York. A wrong turn thanks to an altered sign sends them to the incorrect house, and they find themselves joining six colorful characters and a sinister butler named Peeved (when the butler introduces himself by saying "I am Peeved," George responds by saying "I'm a little ticked off myself"). The other guests included a dentist, a military man, a children's show host, a professional game show contestant, a musician, and an actress. George and Pat are initially in character as the mystery weekend assigned identities of Sherlock Condo and Dr. Whatsit, but once they realize that they are not playing a game, they drop the charade. As the evening unfolds, each of the other guests disappears, with a statuette of blind justice and a newspaper article about the vanished guest's acquittal for a serious crime left behind. In each case, the words "Justice will be done" were scrawled upon the article.

As the house empties, Pat and George learn that all of the guests were, in fact, innocent of the charges levelled against them, and that each wrongly accused person cleared his or her name by using math to prove an alibi. The phrase "And then there were none" is used at the end of the fourth episode, when the last of the guests disappear, and there are numerous other callbacks to Christie's mystery, including the villain wearing a British judge's outfit at the end.

Each *Mathnet* serial taught various mathematical themes, and in "The Case of the Mystery Weekend," patterns were an important plot point. The Mathnet detectives manage to solve the case and rescue the missing guests by noticing trends in the orders of the disappearances, as well as using logical thinking to identify discrepancies. Each of the guests is assigned a room designed in a different color, and the disappearances follow the shades of the color wheel. Not only that, but the times of day when each character was acquitted reflect the order of their kidnapping. "The Case of the Mystery Weekend" is widely regarded by fans as one of the best episodes of a classic series.[6]

* * *

Family Guy: And Then There Were Fewer

Seth MacFarlane's animated television series *Family Guy* opened its ninth season with a double-length 2010 episode titled "And Then There Were Fewer." It features the Griffin family and many other recurring characters on the show being invited to an isolated mansion. When they arrive, it is revealed that the actor James Woods is their host, and he claims to want to make amends for past wrongs. Over the course of the night, classic mystery tropes are spoofed, and Woods and four of the other characters are killed. One recurring character is accused of the crime and arrested. Lois Griffin inadvertently discovers the identity of the real killer, and right before she is also slain, the homicidal baby Stewie Griffin fatally shoots the murderer. In a later episode, the wrongly accused person is cleared, and all of the murdered recurring characters remain dead, with the exception of Woods, who is revived thanks to his celebrity status in a later episode.[7]

A story as iconic as *And Then There Were None* is bound to be parodied more in the future, and it remains to be seen how mystery-comedies will be inspired by Christie's work.

[1] Fred Carmichael, *Any Number Can Die* (Samuel French, 1965), all pages.

[2] Fred Carmichael, *Done to Death* (Samuel French, 1971), all pages.

[3] James McDonald, David Vos, and Robert Gerlach, *Something's Afoot* (Concord Theatricals, 2010), all pages.

[4] "Something's Afoot," *The Internet Broadway* Database, accessed July 6, 2025, https://www.ibdb.com/broadway-production/somethings-afoot-3 842. "Something's Afoot," *The Internet Movie Database*, accessed July 6, 2025, https://www.imdb.com/title/tt0362164/?ref_=fn_all_ttl_1.

[5] *"Mathnet,"* *The Internet Movie Database*, accessed July 6, 2025, https://ww w.imdb.com/title/tt0092401/?ref_=nv_sr_srsg_0_tt_4_nm_4_in_0_q_ma thnet.

[6] "Mathnet | The Case of the Mystery Weekend," *YouTube*, uploaded by Digifangsn, October 14, 2016, https://www.youtube.com/watch?v=uyqq4 BIGMuc.

[7] "And Then There Were Fewer Explained," *Everything Explained Today*,

accessed July 6, 2025, https://everything.explained.today/And_Then_Ther e_Were_Fewer/#google_vignette.

Chapter Forty-One

And Then There Were None's Influence on Horror

(Author's note: portions of this chapter are revised from my article "Agatha Christie: Horror Writer," published on the official Agatha Christie website.)

Agatha Christie has been dubbed "The Queen of Crime." Her name is synonymous with mysteries, and with good reason, but she was not exclusively a crime writer. Though the vast majority of her corpus revolves around detection, her body of work covers multiple genres. Her six romantic novels, published under the pseudonym Mary Westmacott, are less well-known, and she is also a travel writer (*Come, Tell Me How You Live*, and the posthumously compiled *The Grand Tour*). What is perhaps the gravest injustice to Christie's legacy is that her influence on the horror genre has largely gone overlooked.

Christie wrote several horror and supernaturally themed short stories. While her work in these genres is not nearly as famous as that of her work producing crime tales, it has not gone ignored– a few of her horror tales have been adapted for radio, and a few more appeared on television as part of *The Agatha Christie Hour*. Christie's work in horror comprises only a tiny percentage of her entire literary oeuvre, but it deserves further examination.

Several of Christie's short stories contain a genuine (or at least a possible) supernatural element. Most of these stories (though not all) appear together in the British collection *The Hound of Death*, though they are spread across multiple anthologies in the United States. The short story "The Hound of

Death" centers around a nun who may have fantastic powers of premonition and destruction. "The Fourth Man" is a tale of infatuation, jealousy, and death, centered around a woman who might have clung to life after death by inhabiting another woman's body. "The Gypsy" blends premonitions of sudden death and portents of doom with rumors of ghosts that haunt ancient sacred stones. "The Lamp" centers around Mrs. Lancaster (who may or may not be the same character as the "crazy-old-lady-with-a-glass-of-milk" who is a major character in *By the Pricking of My Thumbs*, has a cameo appearance in *Sleeping Murder*, and is referenced in *The Pale Horse*), a woman whose family may be sharing a house with a young ghost. "The Strange Case of Sir Arthur Carmichael" focuses on a man who appears to have switched bodies with a cat. "The Last Séance" is a chilling tale focusing on a grieving mother's attempts to regain contact with her deceased daughter. The story "In A Glass Darkly" revolves around a man who witnesses the specter of a future murder in his mirror. Finally, "The Dressmaker's Doll" is a creepy story about an inanimate object that appears to be moving about of its own free will.

A number of Christie's short stories contain a fleeting reference to something that might or might not be something supernatural. "The Red Signal" and "S.O.S." both hint that some force beyond the known laws of science might have intervened to save a life. The short story collection *The Mysterious Mr. Quin* and the two additional Harley Quin/Mr. Satterthwaite stories outside that anthology feature hints of supernatural activity, but nothing definite. Inspired by the commedia dell'arte character often depicted with the ability to appear and disappear at will, Harley Quin may be an ordinary man who simply inspires Mr. Satterthwaite to act as a detective, brings together couples, and solves crimes. However, some critics believe that Christie implies that Harley Quin often works as a conduit between the worlds of the living and the dead, righting wrongs that the dead left behind and making sure that lovers are happy. At the end of "The Man from the Sea," for example, Mr. Quin speaks as if he is fully aware of the deepest, darkest secrets and desires of a deceased man. Readers can decide whether to view the Harley Quin stories as straight mysteries or mysteries that are tinged with a beneficent supernatural element.

Other Christie stories feature a supposed supernatural element that turns out to be more mundane. In "Wireless," an elderly woman believes that her late husband is trying to contact her. In "The Mystery of the Blue Jar," psychic phenomena are thought to be connected to the titular antique. "The Flock of Geryon" features a cult leader who claims to be able to induce spiritual visions. "The Dream" centers around a man who claims to have seen his own suicide in a nightmare. "The Idol House of Astarte" is about a case where a man may have been stabbed through black magic. "The Blue Geranium" features a medium predicting doom and flowers that change color in a spooky manner. In all of these stories, however, the crime is entirely the work of human criminals who deliberately invoke thoughts of the supernatural in order to distract from their own very clever plots.

Some of Christie's supernatural works are not really horror stories, but instead are religiously themed morality tales. "The Call of Wings," for example, only has a brief hint of the supernatural, particularly at the end, as a wealthy man forsakes all things material in order to follow a more heavenly path. The short anthology *Star Over Bethlehem* contains multiple short stories with Christian themes and supernatural elements such as angels and miracles.

Some of Christie's "horror" stories involve no trace of a supernatural theme. Instead, the horror comes from people being in a perfectly natural, albeit horrifying, position. The evil in these stories comes from purely human means, and everyone involved is completely certain that their terror comes from entirely mortal sources. In this type of horror story, sympathetic (or at least interesting) characters are placed in a horrible but completely natural position that fills them with terror. Examples of these stories include Stephen King's novel *Misery* or Edward Chodorov's classic play *Kind Lady*, where an injured novelist is held hostage by his "biggest fan," and an elderly woman is trapped in her own house by an evil gang that convinces her would-be saviors that the perfectly capable old woman is actually senile, respectively. Christie's short story "Philomel Cottage" can be viewed as a horror story, as a woman is trapped in a house, along with the realization that she may have married a serial killer. Her one-act play, *The Rats,* centers around two people who slowly, terrifyingly realize that they are inexorably caught (like "rats in a trap," hence the title), in a plot to frame them for murder.

Christie's horror and supernatural writing was mainly relegated to short stories, but these themes occasionally appear in her novels. *The Sittaford Mystery* features a faked séance that leads to the discovery of a murder, *Hallowe'en Party* contains a few magical parlor tricks, and *Murder is Easy* contains a sub-sub-sub-plot connected to witchcraft. The supernatural features prominently in only two novels. In *Endless Night*, the curse of Gipsy's Acre appears to be shockingly real as the bodies pile up, and in *The Pale Horse*, three "witches" claim to possess the power to curse people to death, but in both novels, the murders are committed strictly by natural, human means.

While it is not widely seen as a horror novel, *And Then There Were None* has had a significant impact on the horror genre. The trope of a group of people trapped in an isolated place, and are then murdered one by one by a mysterious killer, has become a hallmark of the slasher film genre, but its popularity has origins in *And Then There Were None*. Not only that, but Vera Claythorne, particularly the version of her from Christie's stage adaptation, is widely considered to be the prototype for the "final girl." In many teen horror movies, characters are murdered one by one, but at the end, when the villain is vanquished (at least until the sequel), one young woman is left standing: usually the most virtuous and virginal of the characters. This survivor is commonly referred to as "the final girl." Though the book version of Vera does not qualify for that distinction, the stage and subsequent movie versions likely served as a major inspiration for this trope.

Christie will always be celebrated for her work writing crime stories, but it is important to remember that she worked outside of her trademark genre. Most of her horror short stories were written before the mid-1930s, although her two novels with strong supernatural themes, *The Pale Horse* and *Endless Night*, were both published in the 1960's. Agatha Christie may be the Queen of Crime, but her kingdom extends far beyond the bounds of just mystery fiction.[1]

[1] Chris Chan, "Agatha Christie: Horror Writer?," *The Hone of Agatha Christie*, September 27, 2018, https://www.agathachristie.com/news/2018/agatha-christie-horror-writer.

Chapter Forty-Two

Works Inspired by "And Then There Were None"

Highly successful books tend to spawn imitators, even entire genres. Countless creative works have drawn inspiration from *And Then There Were None* without falling into parody. The idea of "people gathered together in an isolated place, getting killed one by one, often to a set pattern" has become a common trope, with different creators putting their own spins on the premise. *And Then There Were None* not only helped shape the modern horror genre, it has shaped the crime novel as well. There are so many works inspired by *And Then There Were None* that covering all of them would fill a full-length book. This chapter will simply study some of the most prominent examples. As a warning, many spoilers will follow.

* * *

Screen Productions

The House of Fear

The 1933 Sherlock Holmes movie *A Study in Scarlet* may or may not have been a source of inspiration for *And Then There Were None*, but it is likely that Agatha Christie may have influenced the plot of a Sherlock Holmes film. The movie *The House of Fear (1945)* is the tenth movie in the Sherlock Holmes series starring Basil Rathbone and Nigel Bruce as Holmes and Watson, a series which, after the first movie, *The Hound of the Baskervilles*, uses largely original stories for plots, though there are countless references to the original canon. The story combines aspects of *And Then There Were None* with the Holmes story "The Five Orange Pips." In this movie, a group of seven men known as the Good Comrades Club live together in an isolated, spooky house. One by one, they receive envelopes containing a steadily diminishing number of orange pips, matching the number of Good Comrades remaining. Soon after each man receives some pips, that individual is killed in a way that mutilates the body. There is no nursery rhyme, and the motive for the crimes is completely different from Christie's novel, but the trope of a diminishing number of inhabitants in a house is front and center.[1]

* * *

Battle Royale

One of the most controversial of modern Japanese films, 2000's *Battle Royale* takes a disturbing premise. In the wake of youth unrest, a tyrannical Japanese government has decreed that each year, a classful of teenaged students will be brought to an isolated island and forced to kill each other until there is only one survivor. The movie is thought to be an inspiration for *The Hunger Games*.

Aside from the premise of people coming to an island and being killed, it is the ending that most closely mirrors *And Then There Were None*'s play version. A character fakes deaths by shooting, the movie's central antagonist dies in a manner comparable to *And Then There Were None*'s, and by the end, the only characters left standing are a young couple, neither of whom has killed anybody except in justifiable self-defense.[2]

* * *

Mindhunters

The 2004 movie *Mindhunters* takes the basic premise of *And Then There Were None* and adds a lot of grisly scenes. In this film, a team of six young FBI profilers (many of these actors would have regular roles on CBS crime shows in the coming years) go on a weekend trip led by their eccentric instructor. Right before they leave, a stranger working in law enforcement joins them in an observational capacity. Sent to a training facility on a small island owned by the government, they are told that they will be participating in a simulation to catch a fictional serial killer. Over the course of the next few days, a "murderer" will strike multiple times in the simulated small town filled with mannequins. The goal is to develop a full profile of the killer by the end of the weekend.

Pretty soon, they discover a gruesomely arranged dummy, but as they begin to process the scene, they set off a booby trap that leads to the death of one member of the team. As the film progresses, they are picked off through a similar booby traps, all designed to take out a specific person by preying on the target's weaknesses. The deaths are uniformly gory, featuring a living person being flash-frozen and shattered after being sprayed with liquid nitrogen, an exsanguination and decapitation, an impalement with arrows, internal bleeding after consuming acid, a bomb, and some other similarly bloody deaths. Shortly before each death, a broken wristwatch indicates the time when the next death will occur.

In a couple of instances, it is pure chance that the victim managed to die at precisely the predicted moment. In another case, it is practically a miracle that two people were not killed by a trap, and in another instance, a booby trap would not have worked if someone had just taken two steps to either side. None of the victims have done anything to deserve death, and they are being targeted simply because a psychotic person enjoys killing. There is no nursery rhyme linking the means of death, but some elements of the closing scene and one line of dialogue closely mirror the denouement of Christie's play.

Ultimately, most of the characters of *Mindhunters* prove to be rather poor profilers, as they fail to deduce the patterns behind the slaughter before it is too late, and they do not use intelligent reasoning to figure out which one among them is guilty, instead screaming accusations at each other, clutching upon every potential scrap of evidence to cast doubt upon each other, and basically acting as if they have never seen a slasher movie in their lives, as they fail to take elementary precautions. The central character does devise a clever trap to catch the killer, but had she set up her snare a lot earlier, she could have saved most of the characters' lives.

There is some good clueing, as one early scene positions the killer, and how the killer nudges the others into the desired positions like pieces on a chessboard is quite obvious when the viewer watches the movie with an observant and suspicious eye. Other aspects of the movie strain credulity, as one wonders how the killer would have had the time to set up some traps, or how the killer could possibly know that a bomb would not have a larger radius of destruction. What *Mindhunters* lacks in Christie's class and subtlety, it makes up for with darkness and bloody carnage.[3]

* * *

Harper's Island

The 2009 CBS miniseries *Harper's Island* was frequently compared to *And Then There Were None* upon its release, though the narrative is probably more inspired by the slasher genre that may have some roots in *And Then There Were None.* In this series, starring Elaine Cassidy, Christopher Gorham, Katie Cassidy, and Gina Holden, a young couple is getting married at Harper's Island, a popular tourist destination. Harper's Island has a dark past, however, as several years earlier, a madman slaughtered several people before allegedly being slain by the police. After dozens of wedding guests arrive on the island, they are slain "one by one" in various unpleasant ways, at least one and often more per episode. Each of the thirteen episodes takes its title from a sound connected to at least one of the victims' grisly deaths, such as "Whap," "Ka-Blam," "Bang," and "Thrack, Splat, Sizzle." Some of the characters have dark and deadly secrets in their pasts, while others are completely innocent bystanders who definitely do not deserve death. In many cases, the victims seem to be punished for being immature party girls and frat boys. The final confrontation with the killer has strong parallels to Christie's stage version of *And Then Were None*, and in the classic moral tradition of slasher films, the survivors are the only major characters who are never known to have had sex outside of marriage.[4]

* * *

The Hateful Eight

The Kevin Elyot stage adaptation of *And Then There Were None* was billed as "Christie with a Tarantino twist." Quentin Tarantino's 2015 movie *The Hateful Eight* is his own twist on *And Then There Were None.* The movie is a Western where eight individuals with violent pasts are stranded at a snowbound establishment in post-Civil War Wyoming. Though there is rarely any doubt as to who kills whom, the number of people in the cabin dwindles, and some of the deaths are strongly reminiscent of Christie's book, including a shooting near the end, and a final hanging. There is an unspoken moral that all of the characters are receiving karmic punishment for the lives they have taken in the past, and there is a bit of doubt at the end as to whether the number of survivors at the end will be none, one, or two.[5]

* * *

Squid Game

The South Korean phenomenon *Squid Game*, whose first season aired in 2021 on Netflix, has several points of comparison to *And Then There Were None.* A group of people, mostly but not all strangers, are brought to an isolated island, and most of them die. The cast is much bigger, with four hundred fifty-six players in the twisted games, though only about ten (perhaps a bit more depending on who the viewer considers a "main" character) play major roles, and as in Christie's novel, only three of these central characters are women. While hardly any of the characters, with a couple of major exceptions, are killers before they come to the island, they are all linked by being deeply in debt, and they need the prize money in order to survive.

The identity of *Squid Game's* first season's primary villain has many points of characterization and motive with *And Then There Were None's*, including the character's supposed exit from the narrative, general health, and skill at manipulating the proceedings.[6]

* * *

Other Works with a Tenuous Connection

There are other works that are very loosely inspired by *And Then There Were None*. 1970's *Five Dolls for an August Moon* is an Italian thriller where several people visit an island to gain control of a scientist's new invention, and then the characters die one by one. A 1985 pornographic movie (unseen by this author), *Ten Little Maidens*, is allegedly based on Christie's book. *Suspicions* (1995) has six individuals trapped at a cabin in the middle of nowhere to memorialize a friend's death, and they soon start dying. 2014's *Sabotage*, starring Arnold Schwarzenegger, is about shady DEA agents who are trying to get rich off of stolen money. It is sometimes compared to Christie's work, but other than a steadily declining cast, there is no significant parallel to her novel. A 2017 film titled *And Then There Were None*, written and directed by Jantonio Turner, does not even credit Christie as source material. It features eight people in the Mojave Desert, with a lot of deaths. Though several websites claim the movie is based on Christie's book, in reality, the only point of similarity is that the members of the DEA team die one by one, so the connection to Christie's work is very weak. Several of these movies are listed as Christie adaptations on the Internet Movie Database, but given the weaknesses of the connections to the source material, they really should not be.[7]

[1] "The House of Fear (1945)," *The Internet Movie Database*, accessed July 6, 2025, https://www.imdb.com/title/tt0037794/?ref_=fn_all_ttl_1.

[2] "Battle Royale (2000)," *The Internet Movie Database*, accessed July 6, 2025, https://www.imdb.com/title/tt0266308/?ref_=fn_all_ttl_1.

[3] "Battle Royale (2000)," *The Internet Movie Database*, accessed July 6, 2025, https://www.imdb.com/title/tt0266308/?ref_=fn_all_ttl_1.

[4] "Harper's Island (2009)," *The Internet Movie Database*, accessed July 6, 2025, https://www.imdb.com/title/tt1232320/?ref_=fn_all_ttl_1.

[5] "The Hateful Eight (2015)," *The Internet Movie Database*, accessed July 6, 2025, https://www.imdb.com/title/tt3460252/?ref_=fn_all_ttl_1.

[6] "Squid Game (2021-2025)," *The Internet Movie Database*, accessed July 6, 2025, https://www.imdb.com/title/tt10919420/?ref_=fn_all_ttl_1.

[7] "Agatha Christie," *The Internet Movie Database*, accessed July 6, 2025, https://www.imdb.com/name/nm0002005/?ref_=fn_all_nme_1.

Chapter Forty-Three

Television Episodes

Several television epsiodes from both mystery and non-mystery series pay homage to *And Then There Were None* as well.

Frasier – "Give Him the Chair!" (S1E19)

The sitcom *Frasier*, a spinoff of *Cheers*, was not a traditional crime show, but it had a couple of mystery-themed episodes throughout its run, including an episode where Frasier's (Kelsey Grammer) retired police officer father, Martin (John Mahoney), solved a cold case. In Season One, Episode Nineteen, "Give Him the Chair," Frasier resents his father's battered recliner, which clashes with his apartment's décor, so he gives it away, much to his father's rage. When Frasier tracks down the chair and tries to retrieve it, he finds that a local junior high school is using it for their production of *And Then There Were None*. Mrs. Warren (Valerie Curtin), the play's harried director, is frustrated by the lack of talent exhibited by the cast, as well as the ham acting marring the poisoning scene, and is reluctant to return the chair because the shabby piece of furniture is more entertaining than anything else on stage. When the young actor playing Doctor Armstrong takes ill, Mrs. Warren makes a deal with Frasier. If Frasier, who played Doctor Armstrong in a school production decades earlier, will play Armstrong that night, he can have the chair. Frasier obliges, jumping into the role at the last minute.

When Frasier first learns that the play in question is *And Then There Were*

None, he adopts an English accent and quotes, "On the contrary, Major. Many a psychotic killer would appear to be quite normal. You see, you can never suspect that underneath that calm exterior there lies the heart of a maniac, ah-ha-ha." Immediately afterwards, Frasier adds, "Happens to be true, by the way." This line is not in the actual play, and there is no "Major," either.[1]

* * *

Miss Fisher's Murder Mysteries

A 2013 episode of the Australian period crime series *Miss Fisher's Murder Mysteries*, starring Phryne (fry-NAY) Fisher (Essie Davis) as a 1920s private investigator. The final episode of the second season, "Murder Under the Mistletoe," has Miss Fisher and her friends meeting some other characters in an isolated mountain chalet, and people are killed in manners reflecting "The Twelve Days of Christmas."[2]

[1] Anne Flett-Giordano and Chuck Ranberg, *Fraiser*, Season 1, episode 19, directed by James Burrows, featuring Kelsey Grammer, David Hyde Pierce, and John Mahoney, aired March 17, 1994, Paramount, 2003, DVD.

[2] *"Miss Fisher's Murder Mysteries*: "Murder Under the Mistletoe,"" *The Internet Movie Database*, accessed July 6, 2025, https://www.imdb.com/title/tt3140250/?ref_=ttep_ep_13.

Chapter Forty-Four

Books

Countless books draw inspiration and pay direct homage to *And Then There Were None*. These are just a few leading examples.

The Frankenstein Factory

Edward D. Hoch is one of the most prolific and respected American mystery writers, writing numerous series over the course of his career. One of these was the Carl Crader mysteries, a trilogy set in a technologically advanced future. In the third of the Crader books, *The Frankenstein Factory* (1975), Crader only has a brief appearance. In *Frankenstein Factory*, Horseshoe Island off the coast of Mexico is the home of a possibly mad scientist, who is trying to reanimate the dead. When one corpse is brought back to life, the other individuals are killed off one at a time. Is the new "Frankenstein's monster" responsible, or is someone else? The novel is quite open about being a homage to Christie, as it not only mentions her books a couple of times, but most of the characters have names very close to those in *And Then There Were None*. The solution to the mystery, though, is quite different from Christie's.[1]

* * *

The Eleventh Little Indian

Originally published in French in 1979 and translated into English the following year, *The Eleventh Little Indian* by Jacquemard-Sénécal, is a novel that is an open tribute to *And Then There Were None*. A French theater is producing a new adaptation of Christie's classic novel. When the actor playing the murderer arrives a little late, he finds all of his castmates dead of poisoned makeup, plus one additional body of a stranger. Over the course of the book, the actor investigates the crime alongside the official police, and the backstory behind the murder riffs on numerous pivotal aspects and plot points of Christie's work. The ending borrows one of Dame Agatha's most famous solutions from another classic work (after hinting throughout at other classic Christie solutions), but the novel's final sense of justice is closer to Michel Foucault than Agatha Christie.[2]

* * *

The Name of the Rose

The Name of the Rose is one of the most critically respected novels that is inspired in part by *And Then There Were None*. Umberto Eco's acclaimed 1980 novel about a series of murders at an early-fourteenth-century Italian monastery pays homage to many writers. The Franciscan William of Baskerville, the central investigator, is clearly a reference to the classic Sherlock Holmes story. The blind librarian monk Jorge of Burgos is based on the similarly disabled and employed Argentinian writer Jorge Luis Borges (who was not a monk), who was famed as a literary miniaturist known for very short writings and his recurring themes of libraries. Bits of other works of literature are worked into the plot, but the parallel to *And Then There Were None* is often overlooked. Over the course of the book, several monks are killed in manners that reflect the Seven Trumpets from the Biblical book of Revelation. This mirrors the deaths matching the nursery rhyme in Christie's novel.

Unlike Christie's works which uniformly end in a full revelation of truth, and almost always in a triumph for the detective, *The Name of the Rose's* ending reflects a postmodernist bent, where supposed patterns turn out to

231

be purely random (though upon critical analysis, the odds of the coincidences connected to the deaths defy the odds of pure chance, and the conclusion of chaotic randomness seems forced), and the central characters are not left exultant at the end of their adventures. Even though the truth of the matter has been revealed, serious consequences mean that the ending is not a triumphant one for the protagonists.[3]

✳ ✳ ✳

The Decagon House Murders

The Decagon House Murders is an open homage not just to *And Then There Were None*, but to the entire genre of Golden Age mysteries. The author, Yukito Ayatsuji, helped to create the Honkaku Mystery Writers Club, which celebrated the style of classic mystery puzzles that were popular in the early twentieth century. *The Decagon House Murders* was Ayatsuji's first published novel.

The book centers around seven college students who are big fans of mysteries, and they produce a crime fiction magazine titled *Dead Island*, which was the original Japanese title for *And Then There Were None*. The characters go by nicknames, taking the monikers of classic writers, like Ellery Queen, Edgar Allan Poe, Gaston Leroux, S.S. Van Dine, Baroness Orczy, John Dickson Carr, and Agatha Christie, though the personalities of the characters do not particularly match the authors whose names they adopt. The students are responsible for the accidental death of one of their friends, and in the beginning, an unnamed character plots revenge. The seven students are lured to a small island, where a quartet of murders occurred in the recent past. The main structure of the building is the Decagon House, a ten-sided structure with ten rooms. Soon, the friends start dying one by one...

Christie and other Golden Age mystery writers are frequently mentioned and there are numerous allusions to their work.[4]

From 2021 to 2022, the novel was adapted into a five-part manga series.

* * *

An Entire Subgenre

The aforementioned examples are some of the most famous books inspired by *And Then There Were None*, but there are so many "people killed off in an isolated location" novels that it is practically a subgenre now. The recent American edition of the Japanese mystery novel *Death on Gokumon Island* (1947-8) by Seishi Yokomizo, states that the book draws inspiration from *And Then There Were None*. It features mysterious deaths on an island marred by feuding families, and is the second novel to feature the recurring detective Kosuke Kindaichi. Some, like Elizabeth Kan Buzzelli's *And Then They Were Doomed* (2019), part of her Little Library Mystery series, features mysterious goings-on at an Agatha Christie conference in Michigan, where most of the people invited have names straight out of Christie's books, and the protagonist must figure out if someone is trying to replicate *And Then There Were None*, or possibly another of Christie's books…. In another example, Alice Feeney's 2022 novel *Daisy Darker* sees a twisted family slowly being picked off on an island during the matriarch's eightieth birthday celebration. There are many more books inspired by Christie's classic premises, too many to list here, and the subgenre grows larger each year.

[1] Edward D. Hoch, *The Frankenstein Factory* (Mysterious Press.com/Open Road, 2013), Kindle.

[2] Jacquemard-Sénécal, *The Eleventh Little Indian*, (G.K. Hall, 1980), 1-369.

[3] Umberto Eco, translated by William Weaver, *The Name of the Rose*, (HarperVia, 1994), Kindle.

[4] Yukito Ayatsuji, *The Decagon House Murders* (Pushkin Vertigo, 1987, 2021 ed.), Kindle.

Conclusion

And *Then There Were None* was the first Christie novel I ever read. When I was ten, I received a nice black leatherette-bound copy of it for Christmas from a relative, but with no description of it on the cover, I had no idea what the book was about, so I had no interest in it. I left the book on the piano, thinking it was probably a boring book for adults. Soon after school started in January, I realized that having finished the previous book I was reading in school, I needed something else to peruse during that portion of the fifth-grade class day where we were all expected to sit quietly and read. As my mother was hurriedly getting my sister and me ready for school, I grabbed the first book I could find and stuffed it in my backpack. I figured I would find it tedious, but I could bring a more interesting book the next day. That day as we read at our desks, I was enthralled. The novel hooked me right away, and I found it more entertaining than anything else I had read lately. I read most of the book at school, and finished almost all of it that night at home.

Almost all of it. Because as a ten-year-old kid, I assumed that the final chapter featuring the killer's confession was just some boring postscript tacked on by the publishers (I had read a bunch of those in the past and never came across one I would not have been happier skipping), so I did not read it that night. That night, I lay in bed for a long time, trying to answer Sir Thomas Legge's question: *Who killed them?* I had enjoyed the book so much, and I could not understand why Christie would leave the reader hanging like that.

The next day, I brought the book back to school and read it again. Having extra reading time that day, I made it to the final chapter, and *this* time I read it, and as I did, I smacked myself on the forehead for skipping it the previous night.

From that day forward, I was hooked. I raided the school library for more Christie books and begged for more Christie novels for my upcoming birthday and for treats when I was good, which, not to brag, was pretty much all of the time. By September of seventh grade, twenty months after I first read *And Then There Were None,* I had read all of Christie's mystery novels, plus all of the short stories and plays that were available at the time, and her *Autobiography.* I have remained an avid Christie fan ever since, watching all of the adaptations I can find. I love writing essays about Christie's work and legacy, and for a long time, I have wanted to write an entire book about Christie's most popular novel. This book has turned out to be well over ten thousand words longer than Christie's original story!

As I write this in July 2025, I have discovered one more project based on *And Then There Were None.* Games manufacturer Laurence King has released a number of projects, such as jigsaw puzzles, playing cards, and bingo games with themes connected to famous authors, including Christie. After releasing puzzles based on Christie herself, Poirot, and Miss Marple, the fourth puzzle in this series is "The World of Agatha Christie: *And Then There Were None,*" a 1000-piece puzzle with artwork by Ruby Ash, featuring more than forty clues and a guide to the novel. The puzzle is set to be released in September of 2025.[1]

I hope that this book has served to enhance other people's understanding of *And Then There Were None* and its lasting legacy on the broader culture.

—*Chris Chan*

[1] "The World of Agatha Christie: *And Then There Were None,*" *Laurence King,* accessed July 6, 2025, https://www.laurenceking.com/products/the-world-of-agatha-christie-and-then-there-were-none?srsltid=AfmBOooP2 A_HvGCd6CcAepZGqlH-IHpqn4WZeDkRKchqhIELGxOWTKJy.

Bibliography

- Agatha Christie Wiki. Accessed July 4, 2025. https://agathachristie.fandom.com/wiki/.
- "And Then There Were Fewer Explained." *Everything Explained Today*. Accessed July 6, 2025. https://everything.explained.today/And_Then_There_Were_Fewer/#google_vignette.
- "And Then There Were None." TvTropes.org. Accessed July 4, 2025. https://tvtropes.org/pmwiki/pmwiki.php/Literature/AndThenThereWereNone.
- "And Then There Were None (Ten Little Indians) (1968)." *Board Game Geek*. Accessed July 6 2025. https://boardgamegeek.com/boardgame/11387/and-then-there-were-none-ten-little-indians.
- Awe Productions. *Agatha Christie: And Then There Were None*. The Learning Company. CD-ROM. 2005.
- Awe Productions. *Agatha Christie: Evil Under the Sun*. The Learning Company. CD-ROM. 2007.
- Ayatsuji, Yukito. *The Decagon House Murders*. Pushkin Vertigo, 1987, 2021 ed. Kindle.
- Barnard, Robert. *A Talent to Deceive: An Appreciation of Agatha Christie*, Revised and Updated Edition. Mysterious Press, 1987.
- Bennett, Natalie. "Theatre Review: Agatha Christie's *And Then There Were None*." *My London Your London*. December 28, 2005. https://mylondonyourlondon.com/?p=41.
- Birkinshaw, Alan, director. *Ten Little Indians*. Breton Film Productions/Pathe Communications, 1989. 1 hr. 40 min. KI Studio Classics, 2020. DVD.

- Bogart, Paul, Philip F. Falcone, Leo Farrenkopf, and Dan Zampino, directors. *Ten Little Indians*. 1959. 1 hr. Video Yesteryear, 2008. DVD.
- Bristow, Gwen & Bruce Manning. *The Invisible Host*. Dean Street Press, 1930, 2021 ed. Kindle.
- "Buchenwald: The Statistics of Buchenwald." *Jewish Virtual Library*. Accessed July 6, 2025. https://www.jewishvirtuallibrary.org/the-statistics-of-buchenwald.
- "Burgh Island Hotel." Accessed July 3, 2025. https://www.burghisland.com.
- Carmichael, Fred. *Done to Death*. Samuel French, 1971.
- Carmichael, Fred. *Any Number Can Die*. Samuel French, 1965.
- Christie, Agatha. *Agatha Christie: An Autobiography*. HarperCollins, 1977, 2010 ed. Kindle.
- Christie, Agatha. *And Then There Were None*. HarperCollins, 1939, 2009 ed. Kindle.
- Christie, Agatha. *And Then There Were None* (play). In *The Mousetrap and Other Plays*. Harper Collins, 2012. Kindle.
- Christie, Agatha. *And Then There Were None* (play). Samuel French, 1943, 2015 ed.
- Christie, Agatha. *Cards on the Table*. HarperCollins, 1937, 2011 ed. Kindle.
- Christie, Agatha. *Miss Marple: The Complete Short Stories*. HarperCollins, 1985, 2011 ed. Kindle.
- Christie, Agatha. *The Murder of Roger Ackroyd*. HarperCollins 1926, 2011 ed. Kindle.
- Christie, Agatha, François Riviére, and Frank Leclercq. *And Then There Were None* HarperCollins, 2009.
- Christie, Agatha and Joy Wilkinson. *And Then There Were None: A BBC Radio 4 Full Cast Dramatization*. BBC, released 2011. CD.
- Christie, Agatha and Pascal Davoz. *Ils étaient dix*. Paquet, 2020.
- Clair, René, director. *And Then There Were None*. Twentieth Century Fox, 1945. 1 hr., 37 min., https://www.amazon.com/Then-There-Were-None/dp/B08678Z4M1/ref=sr_1_2?crid=3SVU3BNA4YLH&dib

=eyJ2IjoiMSJ9.uzTkKnboKoaiz3i-d5w5zuqqIf3nHWcwAlwI984nP0
QZlMxOmBwVY57aOcikjL3GNZENRfYkcElODEBa8ru2upyiOizG
j7XJtiPogyDLByPcViiqRCgGjhp-guUTemYqxOFhguoPO5Us2DFCi
ExBSm8saLJbmRIXCEpzqCwef-26ElDyrthmuN3k-UdNZvUUwZS
Q1Pwnaiq-pk0jXRPEqgOjbC0FN1iIPyQxwd3hjRg.RoLsZxcgqj1dG
F851obKpJDfFBQ0lSiWk0v5hSS_Kj8&dib_tag=se&keywords=and+
then+there+were+none+1945&qid=1751637574&s=movies-tv&spre
fix=and+then+there+were+none+19%2Cmovies-tv%2C820&sr=1-2.

- Collinson, Peter, director. *Diez Negritos*. Filibuster Films/COMECI/-Coralta Cinematografica, 1974. 1hr. 48 min. Divisa. DVD/Blu-Ray.

- Collinson, Peter, director. *Ten Little Indians*. Filibuster Films/COME-CI/Coralta Cinematografica, 1974. 1hr. 38 min. Scorpion Releasing, 2017. Blu-Ray.

- Curran, John. *Agatha Christie: Murder in the Making*. HarperCollins, 2011. Kindle.

- Curran, John. *Agatha Christie's Secret Notebooks: Fifty Years of Mysteries in the Making*. HarperCollins, 2010. Kindle.

- Eco, Umberto, translated by William Weaver. *The Name of the Rose*. HarperVia, 1994. Kindle.

- Flett-Giordano, Anne and Chuck Ranberg. *Fraiser*. Season 1, episode 19. Directed by James Burrows. Featuring Kelsey Grammer, David Hyde Pierce, and John Mahoney. Aired March 17, 1994. Paramount, 2003, DVD.

- Flynn, Gillian. "Gillian Flynn: 'Agatha Christie blew my mind. Every character was evil." *The Guardian*, July 6, 2018. https://www.theguardi an.com/books/2018/jul/06/books-that-made-me-gillian-flynn.

- Frøsland, Karen. "Nystøyl, Kriminelt kraftfull Agatha Christie-opera." *NRK*. Accessed July 4, 2025. https://www.nrk.no/anmeldelser/anme ldelse_-_and-then-there-were-none_-pa-haugesund-teater-1.163872 06.

- Govorukhin, Stanislav , director. *Desyat Negrityat*. Odessa Film Studio, 1987. 2 hrs. 17 min. DVD.

- Green, Julius. *Agatha Christie: A Life in Theatre: Curtain Up*. Harper-

Collins, 2015. Kindle.

- Hackett, David A., translator. *The Buchenwald Report*. Basic Books, 1995.

- Halvorsen, Mathias. *"And Then There Were None." Mathias Halvorsen*. Accessed July 4, 2025. https://www.mathiashalvorsen.com/work#/ and-then-there-were-none-1/.

- Hoch, Edward D. *The Frankenstein Factory*. Mysterious Press.com/Open Road, 2013. Kindle.

- The Home of Agatha Christie. Accessed July 1, 2025. https://www.agat hachristie.com.

- The Internet Broadway Database. Accessed July 6, 2025. https://www. ibdb.com.

- The Internet Movie Database. Accessed July 3, 2025. https://www.imd b.com.

- Jacquemard-Sénécal. *The Eleventh Little Indian*. G.K. Hall, 1980.

- "Kevin Elyot Archive." University of Bristol. Accessed July 4, 2025. https://www.bristol.ac.uk/theatre-collection/explore/theatre/kevin-elyot-archive/.

- Letter from G.W. Fris to Agatha Christie. April 23rd, 1947. The Agatha Christie Archive.

- Marin, Edwin L., director. *A Study in Scarlet*. KBS Productions, 1933. 1 hr., 12 min. DVD.

- Mathnet | The Case of the Mystery Weekend." *YouTube*. Uploaded by Digifangsn. October 14, 2016. https://www.youtube.com/watch?v=uy qq4BIGMuc.

- McAllister, Pam. "Ten Little Who?" In *The New Beside, Bathtub, and Armchair Companion to Agatha Christie*, edited by Dick Riley & Pam McAllister, 144-145. Ungar Publishing, 1993.

- McDonald, James, David Vos, and Robert Gerlach. *Something's Afoot*. Concord Theatricals, 2010.

- Morgan, Janet. *Agatha Christie: A Biography*. HarperCollins, 1986.

- Morris, Jonathan. "Agatha Christie inspiration Burgh Island for sale at £15m." May 10 2023. https://www.bbc.com/news/uk-england-devon-65542868.

- Nawathe, Raja, director. *Gumnaam*. Prithvi Pictures, 1965. 2 hrs. 31 min. EROS. DVD.
- Neill, Roy William, director. *The 9th Guest*. Columbia Pictures, 1934. 1 hr., 5 min. DVD.
- Nevins, Francis M., Jr. *Royal Bloodline: Ellery Queen, Author and Detective*. Popular Press of Bowling Green State, 1974.
- Pollock, George, dir. *Ten Little Indians*. Tenlit Films Ltd./Towers of London Productions. 1965. 1 hr. 31 min. Warner Archive, 2012. DVD.
- Post, Melville Davisson. "The New Administration" in *The Mystery at the Blue Villa*. Legare Street Press, 2022. Kindle.
- Queen, Ellery. *The Roman Hat Mystery*. Mysterious Press/Open Road, 1929, 2011 ed. Kindle.
- Whitlock, Flint. Buchenwald: Hell on a Hilltop. Cable Publishing, 2013. Kindle.
- "The World of Agatha Christie: *And Then There Were None*," Laurence King. Accessed July 6, 2025. https://www.laurenceking.com/products/the-world-of-agatha-christie-and-then-there-were-none?srsltid=AfmBOoo P2A_HvGCd6CcAepZGqlH-IHpqn4WZeDkRKchqhIELGxOWTKJy.

Acknowledgments

Continued thanks to Shawn Simmons for her belief in my work. Also, warmest regards to my brilliant co-workers and friends who asked to remain anonymous.

About the Author

Chris Chan is a writer, educator, and historian. His true crime articles, reviews, and short fiction have appeared in *The Strand*, *The Wisconsin Magazine of History*, *Mystery Weekly*, *Gilbert!*, Nerd HQ, Akashic Books' *Mondays are Murder* webseries, *The Baker Street Journal*, *The MX Book of New Sherlock Holmes Stories*, *Masthead: The Best New England Crime Stories*, *Sherlock Holmes Mystery Magazine*, and multiple MX andBelanger Books anthologies. He is the creator of the Funderburke and Kaiming mysteries, a series featuring private investigators who work for a school and help students during times of crisis. Funderburke and Kaiming are featured in the novels *Ghosting My Friend*, *She Ruined Our Lives*, and *Well-Behaved Children Seldom Make History*. His first book, *Sherlock & Irene: The Secret Truth Behind "A Scandal in Bohemia,"* was published in 2020 by MX Publishing, and he is also the author of the comedic novels *Sherlock's Secretary* and *Nessie's Nemesis*, and the anthology *Of Course He Pushed Him and other Sherlock Holmes Stories* as well as a study on neurodivergence in the media: *The Autistic Sleuth*. His nonfiction mystery criticism series features *Murder Most Grotesque: The Comedic Crime Fiction of Joyce Porter* and *Some of My Best Friends are Murderers: Critiquing the Columbo Killers* (both from Level Best Books). His work has been nominated for the Anthony Award, the Macavity Award, the Derringer Award, long-listed for the Dagger Award, twice nominated for the Agatha Award, four times nominated for the Silver Falchion Award, and won the Best Indie Book Award.

AUTHOR WEBSITE:

https://chrischancrimeandcriticism.blogspot.com

SOCIAL MEDIA HANDLES:

X/Twitter: @GKCfan

Facebook: https://www.facebook.com/chris.chan.7374/

Instagram: https://www.instagram.com/chan3589/

Also by Chris Chan

Non-fiction literary criticism:

Sherlock & Irene: The Secret Truth Behind "A Scandal in Bohemia" (2020, MX Publishing)

Murder Most Grotesque: The Comedic Crime Fiction of Joyce Porter (2021, Level Best Books)

The Autistic Sleuth (2024, MX Publishing)

Some of My Best Friends are Murderers: Critiquing the Columbo Killers (2024, Level Best Books)

Novels:

Sherlock's Secretary (2021, MX Publishing)

Ghosting My Friend (2023, Level Best Books)

Nessie's Nemesis (2023, MX Publishing)

She Ruined Our Lives (2024, Level Best Books)

Well-Behaved Children Seldom Make History (2025, Level Best Books)

Teachers Who Hate Students (2026, Level Best Books)

Short Story Collections:

Of Course He Pushed Him (2022, MX Publishing)

156 Homicides: A Year of Murder in Milwaukee (2026, Level Best Books)

Poetry:

Sherlock Poems (2025, MX Publishing)